"The NAACP
Comes of Age"

BLACKS IN THE DIASPORA

Darlene Clark Hine, John McCluskey, Jr.,
and David Barry Gaspar

General Editors

Kenneth W. Goings

"The NAACP Comes of Age"

THE DEFEAT OF JUDGE JOHN J. PARKER

INDIANA UNIVERSITY PRESS
Bloomington and Indianapolis

Portions of chapter 2 were originally published as chapter 6 in *Developing Dixie: Modernization in a Traditional Society*, W. B. Moore, Jr., J. F. Tripp, and Lyon G. Tyler Jr., eds. (Contributions in American History, No. 127, Greenwood Press, Inc., Westport, Connecticut, 1988), pp. 73–90. Copyright © 1988 by Winfred B. Moore, Jr., Joseph F. Tripp, and Lyon G. Tyler, Jr. Used with permission.

The paper used in this publication meets the minimum requirements of American National Standard for Information Sciences—Permanence of Paper for Printed Library Materials, ANSI Z39.48-1984.

Manufactured in the United States of America

Library of Congress Cataloging-in-Publication Data

Goings, Kenneth W.
    The NAACP comes of age : the defeat of Judge John J. Parker / Kenneth W. Goings.
        p.   cm. — (Blacks in the diaspora)
    Includes bibliographical references.
    ISBN 0-253-32585-4 (alk. paper)
    1. National Association for the Advancement of Colored People. 2. Parker, John J. 3. United States. Supreme Court—Officials and employees—Selection and appointment—History—20th century. 4. Judges—United States—Selection and appointment—History—20th century. 5. Civil rights movements—United States—History—20th century. I. Title. II. Series.
E185.61.G56   1990
342.73'085—dc20
[347.30285]   89-46011
                                                             CIP

1 2 3 4 5 94 93 92 91 90

To my mother, Mary Elizabeth Goings,
and
to the memory of my father,
Harold Raymond Goings

CONTENTS

ACKNOWLEDGMENTS

One of the nicest facets of publishing a book is that one can then publicly thank those who have supported and given assistance to the author. And in my case I owe a great deal of thanks.

First, I would like to acknowledge the National Endowment for the Humanities Summer Seminars for College Teachers. Having always taught at liberal arts colleges, I truly appreciated the opportunity to work at universities with fine research libraries. August Meier directed my first NEH Seminar at Kent State University. Professor Meier is also responsible for helping me select the topic. He and Elliot Rudwick gave invaluable criticisms and insights based upon their enormous knowledge of the field. Otis Graham directed my second NEH Seminar at Stanford University and helped with the New Deal material. Two colleagues from my NEH Seminars who read and gave me valuable comments on my work were Daryl Paulson and Henry Sirgo.

The College of Wooster awarded me two research leaves which greatly assisted my project. But I am even more thankful for my colleagues' support. Helen Osgood gave the manuscript an extensive critical reading just as my spirits were flagging. John Gates and Jim Hodges read various chapters and draft selections, always giving helpful comments. Jean Shunk typed and retyped the manuscript, almost always cheerfully. Hayden Schilling, Erika Laquer, John Hondros, Karen Taylor, Floyd Watts, and James Turner had to listen to Parker "talk" until their ears were ready to burst. I thank them for their patience.

The staff of the Southern Historical Collection at the University of North Carolina at Chapel Hill, particularly Richard Shrader, was always helpful with my use of the Parker papers. The staff of the Library of Congress Manuscript Division, where the NAACP papers are housed, was also of great assistance. In addition I would like to thank the staffs of the Herbert Hoover Presidential Library, the Franklin D. Roosevelt Presidential Library, and the Dwight D. Eisenhower Presidential Library for their assistance.

Rhodes College has given me support from a Faculty Development Endowment Grant to complete the last details of the manuscript, and I am grateful.

I also need to acknowledge a whole gang of friends who buoyed my spirits during the rough times: Eugene O'Connor, Dan Rice, John Sitton, Earl Beverly, Tony Windsor, Karen Dugger, and Dave Beatty. Lastly, a special thanks to Darlene Clark Hine, whose chance encounter with me at the Library of Congress put me onto her co-edited series at Indiana University Press.

As much as I would like to blame someone else for any errors, alas, they are all mine.

From highlighting the brutal crime of lynching in the late nineteenth and early twentieth centuries and protesting discrimination in New Deal and World War II agencies to working for a desegregated society through the Brown decision and the 1964 Civil Rights Act, the National Association for the Advancement of Colored People has a history of notable achievements. Books, articles, and symposia have already focused on these developments. However, one remarkable accomplishment has never received much attention: the work of the Association in defeating the confirmation of Judge John J. Parker's nomination to the U.S. Supreme Court in 1930.

The actual campaign to block Parker from gaining a seat on the High Court lasted only six weeks, but as it was played out on several different levels, it was instrumental in solidifying the position of the organization in the eyes of black and white America. This campaign represents one of the most important chapters in the history of the NAACP. Besieged by critics, black and white, and sapped of money and membership by the Great Depression, the campaign against Parker became a rallying point for the Association that reinvigorated it after the aimlessness following the collapse of its efforts in support of the Dyer Anti-Lynching Bill. Members of the Association received valuable experience in lobbying and organizing that helped make future successes possible. The confirmation debate in the Senate (on Parker's nomination) reveals that the issue of race in national politics which had been ignored after Reconstruction could no longer be overlooked.

Contemporary observers as well as recent historians have downplayed the issue of race in the defeat of Parker's nomination. Instead they have emphasized labor's objections, Parker's conservatism, the "political nature" of the appointment, and divisions within the Republican party. Increasingly, as the debate wore on, the issue of race came to the forefront, and it became as important as, if not more important than, any other factor in Parker's defeat. The NAACP fight against Parker energized black people politically to a degree not seen since the 1860s, and along with other forces, including hostility from the Republican party, it prepared the way for the black voter switch which took place in 1936 with the entry of black people into the New Deal coalition.

The follow-up attempt to defeat the senators who voted for Parker in 1930 indicated the maturity of the NAACP. Activities related to the campaign against pro-Parker senators brought about a need for "new" structures in the organization. Unable to run all of its activities from a central location, the national office of the Association had to reestablish state conferences to coordinate the activities of branches in key states. And again, these state-level campaigns gave current and future leaders experience in political tactics and demonstrated the value of the Association to black people.

Newspaper editorials, politicians, and contemporary social scientists criticized the Association for its work in the defeat of Parker, believing that he would have been a "friend of the race" on the Court. Some current historians echo these thoughts. Although Parker never became a justice of the United States Supreme Court, and therefore we cannot know how he would have ruled, he remained a senior judge of the Fourth Circuit Court for another quarter of a century. Some of the most important civil rights cases occurred during these years. An examination of Parker's decisions reveals that while he was not the stereotypical southern racist judge, he could never fully come to accept the new era ushered in by the *Brown* decision.

The successful NAACP campaign against Judge Parker's confirmation provided inspiration and determination that helped lead the Association to some of its greatest victories. Indeed, with the Parker fight, the Association had "come of age."

"The NAACP Comes of Age"

1.

ORIGINS OF THE NAACP

Prelude to the Parker Fight

From the end of Reconstruction to the founding of the NAACP, the fortunes of black Americans were in steady decline. The Compromise of 1876 which ended the presidential election deadlock marked the official abandonment by the North and the national Republican party of the "children of Lincoln." Once more left to the wiles and wishes of the South, blacks were returned to a quasi-slavery system that the Civil War had supposedly destroyed. Relegated to sharecropping and tenancy, black farmers helped produce the materials, especially cotton, to fuel the industrial expansion continuing in the North and overseas.

One possible source of disruption of the South's "new economic order" was the party known as the Populists. Some whites as well as the blacks who were excluded from the economic rewards of the New South decided that, indeed, it would be necessary to organize on the basis of occupation (not race) in order to gain some control over their lives. The Populists were initially successful in electing members to state legislatures and county commissions and beginning the process of redress for many of the region's shortcomings. However, as with most successful or even semi-successful interracial movements in the South, the Populists were red-shirted with the cry of "black supremacy" by the Democrats. It was an immensely successful attack, and by the early 1890s white "progressives" in the South disdained the cause of black advancement.

The breakup of the "radical" Populists began with the legal disfranchisement campaigns which would reduce the black vote in the South to very meager numbers by World War I. The South was able to disfranchise so easily because white citizens of the North either agreed with them or were indifferent. Racism dominated every aspect of American society. Scholars justified the inferior social status of blacks in works such as U. B. Phillips's *American Negro Slavery*, which informed the American public that blacks had been happy under slavery and were lost without the guidance of their masters. Biologists "proved" that black people were just one step away from the apes they "resembled," and what kind of social-economic progress had the simians made? In the realm of theology, Social Gospellers claimed that those who were wealthy had God's blessings; those who were poor and downtrodden were being punished for their imperfect souls. The idea of Manifest Destiny enabled the United States to extend these principles beyond California to the Philippines with a backstep to Hawaii— ostensibly to help our "little brown brothers" there, but also to acquire a coaling station for our warships so that we could continue to help our "little brown brothers" in the Philippines.

More devastating for black Americans was a set of Supreme Court decisions that would take almost sixty years to overturn. The Civil Rights Law of 1875, ineffective at best, had been a last sop to Republican consciences before the 1876 Compromise. The law at least had some symbolic value, but in 1883, the Court invalidated it. In 1890, Mississippi set up a poll tax and literacy requirement which were upheld by the Court. The Court's most damaging decision for black people was the 1896 decision in *Plessy v. Ferguson*, in which the Court ruled that it was legal to segregate black people as long as their segregated conditions were "equal." By the end of the nineteenth century, the second-class citizenship of black Americans had been reinforced by scholars in the fields of social science, biology, and theology, and by the needs of U.S. foreign policy, by state legislatures, and by the highest court of the land. The result was an increase of violence in the South and occasionally in the North in an attempt to control black people. Lynching and riots were the worst expressions of racial tension. As Table

1 indicates, the number of lynchings that occurred in the more than half a century from 1882 to 1954 was staggering.

In August 1908, a race riot in Abraham Lincoln's hometown of Springfield, Illinois, helped plant the seed which later sprouted into the NAACP.[1] The riot lasted two days. During that time, two blacks were lynched, six were killed, and more than 4,200 militiamen had to be called in to restore order. The white liberal press led by Oswald Garrison Villard, grandson of William Lloyd Garrison and head of the *New York Evening Post*, was appalled. Also appalled was William English Walling,

TABLE 1
Number of Lynchings by Year, 1882–1954

1882	49	1906	62	1930	20
1883	53	1907	58	1931	12
1884	51	1908	89	1932	6
1885	74	1909	69	1933	24
1886	74	1910	67	1934	15
1887	70	1911	60	1935	18
1888	69	1912	61	1936	8
1889	94	1913	51	1937	8
1890	85	1914	51	1938	6
1891	113	1915	56	1939	2
1892	161	1916	50	1940	4
1893	118	1917	36	1941	4
1894	134	1918	60	1942	6
1895	113	1919	76	1943	3
1896	78	1920	53	1944	2
1897	123	1921	59	1945	1
1898	101	1922	51	1946	6
1899	85	1923	29	1947	1
1900	106	1924	16	1948	1
1901	105	1925	17	1949	3
1902	85	1926	23	1950	1
1903	84	1927	16	1951	1
1904	76	1928	10	1952	0
1905	57	1929	7	1953	0
				1954	0

Source: Harry A. Ploski and Warren Marr, II, eds., *The Afro-Americans* (New York: The Bellwether Co.), pp. 275–76.

a wealthy southern reporter who, with his wife, traveled to
Springfield to investigate the riot. Walling then wrote an article
entitled "The Race War in the North," in which he condemned
the public for ignoring atrocities against blacks and questioned
whether or not democracy could survive if this kind of law-
lessness continued. A reader of the article was Mary White
Ovington, herself a descendant of abolitionists and a social
progressive. She was moved by the article and corresponded
with Walling. Weeks later she attended a lecture by Walling
in which he compared race relations in the United States to
conditions in Russia and found the former to be worse. He
had already had the idea of an interracial organization to fight
for "equality," and Ovington pushed him to put his ideas into
action. In the first week of January 1909, Ovington and the
Wallings planned to meet in Walling's apartment with Dr. Henry
Moskowitz, a social worker, and Charles Edward Russell, a
socialist writer friend of Walling, but Russell was unable to
attend.

At their first meeting, the group set Lincoln's birthday as
the start of their efforts to redress the wrong inflicted on black
people, and Oswald Garrison Villard was invited to join. Soon
other members were added. Bishop Alexander Walters of the
African Methodist Episcopal Zion Church made the group interracial. Other early members included Florence Kelley, a progressive associated with Jane Addams through Hull House and
a specialist in labor affairs, and Lillian Wald, another progressive
who ran a settlement house in New York City.

On Lincoln's birthday, the group issued "The Call" (see Ap-
pendix A). "The Call" described the conditions then being faced
by black people, reiterated the legal discrimination which was
taking place, and then called for the political and civil rights
needed to redress racial injustice. Significantly, the manifesto
did not speak to economic solutions. "The Call" received little
attention, even from the black press. Villard then moved to
implement a national conference which "The Call" had antici-
pated. After much debate, the group, which still met in Walling's apartment, settled on "The National Negro Committee"
as the name of their new organization. Plans for "A Conference
on the Status of the Negro" were finalized for May 31 to June
1, 1909. They sent out a thousand invitations. Villard asked

his uncle, William Lloyd Garrison, Jr., to preside. Garrison was too ill but wrote a message to be read to the delegates. Other sponsors and delegates were solicited with a heavy emphasis on people from the old abolitionist families.

Also invited to the conference were the leaders of two strongly opposed factions within black America, Booker T. Washington and W. E. B. Du Bois. By inviting both of them and their supporters and hoping that only Du Bois would show up, white progressives were really signalling their displeasure and impatience with Washington's accommodationist approach, while embracing Du Bois's protest and agitation strategy. Washington, who had been the preeminent black leader through the turn of the century, had suffered a number of setbacks to his policies, including the continued violence inflicted upon blacks. Principal among these events that strongly affected liberal white opinion and confirmed Du Bois's view of Washington were the Atlantic riot in 1906, the Brownsville incident, and the Springfield riot in 1908.

These examples of continued racial violence directed at black people only confirmed for neo-abolitionists the failure of Washington's policy. Indeed, while black people were improving their education and financial capabilities as the Washington philosophy advocated, they were steadily losing ground in the area of political rights. Cooperation with southern moderates no longer seemed productive, a view Du Bois had been advocating for a considerable time.[2]

While Washington's star was on the wane, Du Bois's was on the ascendancy. In 1903, Du Bois published *The Souls of Black Folks*, which contained his public rebuke to Washington and his policies. The increase in violence and denial of civil rights only reinforced in the minds of the "neo-abolitionists" the need for protest and agitation. Several of the founding members of the NAACP were familiar with Du Bois before the initial conference in 1909. In July 1905, Du Bois had founded the Niagara movement, after a "unity" conference sponsored by Villard between the followers of Du Bois and Washington failed because the Washington delegates were intent on controlling the Committee of Twelve (a group set up to help guide black actions).

The Niagara movement demanded enfranchisement, educa-

tion, and the end of race-based distinctions. Mary White Ovington attended the 1906 annual meeting of the Niagara movement
as a reporter for Villard's *Post*, and she also attended the 1906
meeting of Washington's Negro Business League. Her sympa-
thies were clearly with Du Bois. Because of her reporting in
1907, she became the only white person to be invited to join
the Niagara movement. Her support of Du Bois was really
a portent of the support he would receive from the other "neo-
abolitionists" by the time of the 1909 conference. With this
as a background, Villard wrote Washington inviting him to
the conference but providing him with an excuse not to attend.
Washington took the excuse and the matter was settled for
the time being.

About three hundred people attended the conference.[3] Prominent philosophers, anthropologists, economists, and others attended with a view toward dismantling the racial stereotypes
perpetuated by the educational, religious, and political institutions of white America during the last quarter of the nineteenth
century. The conference decided to establish a permanent
organization with a publicity bureau and press section, a
legal bureau, a political and civil rights bureau, an education
department, an industrial bureau, and a "board" to oversee
the organization. A Committee of Forty was appointed to continue the work started by the conference. In an attempt to
get a harmonious group, Washington and some of his most
severe critics were not included. The response by the white
press was somewhat positive; the black press, especially those
newspapers controlled by Washington, was critical.[4]

To get the new organization on its feet and to reduce potential
divisiveness, invitations were sent to John E. Milholland, head
of the Constitution League, a political rights group working
for black people, and to Du Bois for the Niagara movement.
Milholland, who had unsuccessfully attempted to merge his
group early in 1909, was happy to dissolve his organization.
The Constitution League had never really taken off, and he
was its main source of financial support. The Niagara movement, founded in 1905, had always been in rocky shape. In
1907, fellow member and radical William Monroe Trotter broke
with Du Bois, and the organization just limped along until
1909. Moreover, the house organ of the Niagara movement,

The Horizon, had run up a sizeable debt with few readers to sustain it. Like Milholland, Du Bois was ready to dissolve his organization in favor of the National Negro Committee.

In 1910, the second annual conference of the National Negro Committee was held from May 12 to 14. A final planning meeting on May 5 decided on a theme, "The Relationship between Labor Unions and Blacks," and recommended a new name: "The National Association for the Advancement of Colored People." The organization was to consist of a national committee of one hundred, with an executive committee of thirty, with headquarters in New York City. The pre-conference planners also discussed costs of membership and the purpose of meetings. The activities of the NAACP were to include legal aid, mass meetings, investigations of injustices, and publicity.

The second annual conference convened as scheduled on May 12 with Moorfield Storey as president, William English Walling as chairman of the executive committee, Frances Blascoer as executive secretary, John Milholland as treasurer, and Oswald Garrison Villard as assistant treasurer. The conference accepted all the major recommendations of the planners. Du Bois was hired as a paid chairman of the executive committee. Within weeks, the position of chairman of the executive committee was split: Frances Blascoer, executive secretary, assumed all administrative responsibility, and Du Bois became director of publicity and research. Arrangements for Du Bois's appointment were completed on June 28, and fourteen former members of the Niagara movement were added to the committee of one hundred. Du Bois left Atlanta and started on his first project, the publication of *The Crisis.* As the memberships of the two organizations merged, so did the two readerships.Subscribers to *The Horizon* would have their subscriptions fulfilled with issues of *The Crisis,* the first of which was published in November 1910.

Washington was obviously upset by the NAACP's challenge to his leadership as well as by the defection of the neo-abolitionists from his camp. Initially, because he did not want to offend the neo-abolitionists, some of whom had been great supporters in the past (the Garrison family, for example), Washington's critiques were polite and restrained. The fledgling National Negro Committee, unsure of its strength in the black community or the sympathetic white community, responded to Washington's barbs in the same polite and restrained manner. However, as the NAACP continued to grow, the mutual attacks became more harsh. Washington never reconciled with the organization and opposed it until his death in 1915.[5]

After the death of Washington, Du Bois suggested that the Association invite equal numbers of Washingtonians and members of the NAACP to a reconciliation conference at Amenia, New York.[6] To a large extent it was a success: the participants discussed politics, education, industry, discrimination against blacks, and a future program which followed the way of Du Bois more than that of Washington. The NAACP grew in membership and leadership. One of the participants in the Amenia Conference was James Weldon Johnson, considered a "Washington man," although he was a member of the NAACP. By the end of 1916, he was a branch organizer for the Association under Royal Freeman Nash, executive secretary until 1917, and John R. Shillady, executive secretary until 1920. In 1920, Johnson became acting secretary and was then executive secretary until January 1931.[7] Also joining the national office shortly after Johnson was Walter White. Like Johnson, White was from the South, middle class, and a graduate of Atlanta University. Together they helped make the transition from white leadership to black leadership in the secretariat.[8]

Another major staff appointment before the end of the first decade was Herbert J. Seligman, as director of publicity in 1919. Seligman, a reporter for the *New York Evening Post*, had investigated lynching in the South for the organization, and his public relations skills were an enormous asset to the Association. With this staff in place, the Association launched its first major campaign, the fight to secure a federal anti-lynching law. The attempt to secure the Dyer Anti-Lynching Bill lasted from 1919 to 1923 and, while unsuccessful, it provided valuable lessons for the organization and publicized the crime of lynching.

Lynching and mob violence had been a focal point of the NAACP from its earliest days, and increasingly, as the first decade of the Association's existence wore on, more and more resolve was building to do something about the problem. In 1912, the Association, besides continuing its investigations and publicity on lynchings, published *Notes on Lynching in the United*

States.[9] By 1914, the NAACP had become more political and questioned prospective members of Congress on their attitudes toward different race concerns, including lynching. In 1915, Philip G. Peabody, a Boston philanthropist, pledged (but later recanted) $10,000 if the NAACP could come up with a solution to lynching. A Committee on Anti-Lynching Programs was set up to this end, but Peabody rejected their program as not feasible. However, he did donate $1,000 to the anti-lynching account which by 1917 had grown to $9,131. That year, the Association took two major actions in its anti-lynching campaign. First, it hired Lily H. Hammond, wife of a past president of Paine College, to investigate lynchings in the South, supposedly as a reporter for the *Sunday Evening Post.* Second, it decided to spend the money in the anti-lynching account in hopes of getting some momentum going on a solution for this problem. Five thousand dollars would be spent on investigations, $2,500 for propaganda, and $2,000 for prosecution of mob participants.

During World War I, the Association tried to get the federal government to take up the cause of anti-lynching as a way to make the homefront more secure. President Woodrow Wilson was unsympathetic. Combined with lack of support from the White House was an incident which involved black soldiers of the Twenty-fourth Infantry stationed in Houston. Tensions in the city were rising over the issue of black men with arms. On August 23, 1917, a black soldier was arrested for trying to protect another black soldier and a black woman from the police; black soldiers attacked the town. Nineteen people—seventeen whites and two blacks—were killed. Sixty-three soldiers were arrested and thirteen were hanged before the Association could effectively intervene. The NAACP hired A. J. Houston (Sam's son) to defend the remaining soldiers: fifty-one received life sentences; four, long-term sentences; and five, the death penalty. James Weldon Johnson was able to speak to President Wilson, who agreed to look into the matter. Not until 1957, however, was the last soldier released.

Propaganda against lynching was a major strategy for the NAACP, and in 1918 some results were evident. Leonidas Dyer (R-Missouri—a district south of St. Louis) and Merritt Moore (R-Indiana—Indianapolis) introduced anti-lynching bills in Congress. The Dyer bill, which the Association chose to support,

was based on the Fourteenth Amendment and specified that
lynching victims were denied "equal protection" under the law
because the state governments refused to act against the crime
of lynching. The Dyer bill provided that officials knowing of
or being part of lynch mobs could be penalized five years in
prison and/or a $5,000 fine. Mob participants and their sympa-
thizers would be barred from federal juries and could be prose-
cuted. The Moore bill was seen as a step backward since it
only called for investigation and study of the problem, something the Association had been doing for a decade. The same
year, Walling and his Anti-Lynching Committee wanted and
received approval from the board for a national conference on
lynching to help publicize Dyer's efforts as well as to increase
pressure on Congress.

In April 1919, the Association published *Thirty Years of Lynching in the United States, 1889–1919,* and in May, the national
conference was held. The Association was careful to maintain
its nonpartisan role by inviting both Republicans and Democrats, as well as reformers from other movements. Speakers
in addition to the Association's president, Moorfield Storey,
were Chief Justice Charles Evans Hughes, ex-Alabama Governor Emmett O'Neal, General John H. Sherburner of the Ninety-
second Division (a black unit), and Ann Howard Shaw of the
National American Woman's Suffrage Association. Twenty-five
hundred people attended the conference, and it was seen as
a great success. The Association received good publicity in both
the black and white presses for its efforts against lynching.
An indication of just how rampant mob violence was in the
United States and how much need there was for stronger laws
was demonstrated in a dramatic way a few months later. In
August 1919, John R. Shillady, secretary of the Association,
was in Texas trying to publicize its work. He was denied meetings with the governor and attorney general. He did meet with
the acting attorney general, after which he was detained by
the police and jeered in a secret court of inquiry. Then, as
he tried to see the Austin NAACP branch president, he was
beaten by a mob which included a county judge! The governor
supported the mob. The need for a federal law against mob
crimes was beyond all doubt.

In 1919, Dyer's bill H.R. 259 and a companion piece, H.R.

319, calling for a congressional inquiry, were introduced. Charles Curtis (R-Kansas) also introduced a bill calling for the investigation of the problem of lynching, but the Association saw that as a delaying tactic and chose not to support it. It was not until the next year that the House Judiciary Committee finally held hearings on the bill. Dyer and Association witnesses appeared before the committee. In 1920, the Association, through James Weldon Johnson, tried to get Republican candidate Warren G. Harding's support. Harding made some vague promises but never really came through with any help. Dyer had to reintroduce his bill in the next session, as H.R. 13. The delay and diversionary tactics, such as more bills aimed at the investigative approach, did not dampen either Dyer's or the Association's efforts. In the fall of 1921, the House Judiciary Committee "favorably" ordered the bill out. Finally, debate was set for January 25, 1922. The House had to round up enough members to make a quorum, which was finally accomplished, and the bill passed the House on January 26: 231 to 119. However, the battle was still only half won.

The bill was then sent to the Senate where senior Republicans William Borah (R-Idaho), Henry Cabot Lodge (R-Massachusetts), and James E. Watson (R-Indiana) individually and collectively delayed the process, often on the pretext that other work was more urgent. When the bill did come up for debate, it was put into the hands of an inexperienced senator, Samuel Shortridge (R-California), while the Republican heavyweights, including Lodge, retired from the scene of the battle. Shortridge was no match for southern Democrats who kept the bill bottled up throughout the *third* session of the Sixty-seventh Congress. At the end of the session, the Republicans met to decide what their priorities should be for the extraordinary fourth session, which was to run from December 4, 1922, to March 3, 1923. Their list of legislative priorities did not include the anti-lynching bill. The bill would have to be reintroduced in the Sixty-eighth Congress and the process started all over again. For the time being, it was effectively killed. The Association was disheartened. Both Johnson and Walter White had campaigned intensively over the four years of the legislative struggle. The lessons learned and the contacts made by White would hold the Association in good stead in its next major bout involving Congress.[10]

The period from 1923 to 1930 was a time of questioning for the Association. As it continued its legal programs and other activities, it searched for a new direction. The Republicans pursued their lily-white approach to politics, which the Association tried to counter. Meanwhile, black nationalists, especially Marcus Garvey and A. Philip Randolph, sharply criticized the NAACP. Despite these trials and tribulations, the Association had some success in its first two decades of opposition to the laws that imposed an inferior status on black citizens. It sought redress in the state and federal judicial systems.

The first legal case handled by the Association was the Pink Franklin case in 1910.[11] Pink Franklin was a South Carolina sharecropper who had left his tenancy while owing money to the landowner. Franklin then got a tenancy on another farm at which time the first farmer served an arrest warrant against him. In the process of arresting Franklin, the police charged his home, shots were fired, and an officer died. Franklin was charged with murder. He was found guilty and given a death sentence—a sentence upheld by the U.S. Supreme Court. With cooperation from Booker T. Washington, the NAACP was able to get the governor of South Carolina to commute the sentence to life. The case was reopened in 1915, and Franklin received a parole in 1919. Because of this case, the legal department of the Association was firmly established as a working entity.

Another important early legal case involved Steve Greene.[12] Greene, a tenant farmer from Arkansas, left his tenancy after his rent was doubled. The owner forbade him to work in the county ever again. Greene, however, got another job in the county, and his previous employer, furious, rode over to his new place of employment and shot him several times. Greene was able to get to his home, get a gun, and kill his attacker. He fled the state, finally arriving in Chicago, where he was apprehended by the police on a trumped-up, petty larceny charge. When he was questioned about the incident in Arkansas, he attempted suicide. An effort to extradite him back to Arkansas failed when Ida Wells-Barnett intervened and secured his return to Chicago, where he was freed because of a technicality in his extradition papers. Greene then fled to Canada.

In 1910 the Association undertook a third legal case—the case of Thomas Williams. Williams was accused of murdering an eleven-year-old white girl in Asbury Park, New Jersey. There was talk of lynching him. The NAACP intervened and secured his release because of lack of evidence. Williams was then rearrested on a spurious electioneering charge. While in jail, he was given the third degree to secure a confession. The NAACP presented these facts to a congressional committee.[13] It should be noted that these cases were not technically handled by the NAACP, but rather through lawyers secured by the organization. This continued until 1913 when a legal staff was hired. These cases were important, not only because they secured the release of innocent people but because the NAACP gained publicity which informed black people that the Association was working for them.

Besides the legal cases involving criminal charges against individuals, in 1915 the NAACP began its great work in the constitutional cases, chiefly but not exclusively concerned with the implementation and enforcement of the Fourteenth and Fifteenth Amendments. By 1930, the Association through its legal counsel had argued or been party to seven cases before the Supreme Court, winning five of them. The first of these cases was *Guinn v. U.S.*, in which the Association filed an amicus curiae brief on behalf of the United States. The case involved Oklahoma's "grandfather clause," and the Association was able to get the solicitor general of the United States to file against Oklahoma's law. Moorfield Storey, distinguished Boston lawyer and first president of the NAACP, filed the amicus curiae brief for the Association. In 1910 Oklahoma had adopted an amendment to its constitution exempting from its literacy test all people "who, on January 1, 1866, or at any time prior thereto, were entitled to vote under any form of government or who at that time resided in some foreign nation, and their lineal descendants. . . ." The government argued and the Court agreed that this amendment had created or rather recreated the exact situation which the Fifteenth Amendment had been designed to prevent.[14] The law was ruled unconstitutional based on its violation of the Fifteenth Amendment. Although the Association was only a "friend of the Court" in this case, *Guinn v. U.S.* marked a major and important decision for the Association and its constituency.

The next Supreme Court case involving the NAACP concerned residential segregation by ordinance, *Buchanan v. War-ley*.[15] Residential segregation by ordinance meant that the municipality would be a partner in enforcing a deed agreement restricting the owner of a property from selling to anyone who could not because of municipal segregation laws occupy the property. The case started in 1910 when Baltimore passed its first of three residential segregation ordinances. The first two were struck down by court actions taken by the Baltimore branch. Indeed, the impetus for organizing the Baltimore branch lay with the introduction of these ordinances, which made de jure the already de facto residential situation and signaled the hardening of race lines in the country. Decision on the third ordinance was delayed to see what the Supreme Court would do in the *Buchanan v. Warley* case, which involved a residential segregation ordinance in Louisville, Kentucky. In Louisville, Joel Spingarn, chairman of the board of directors, and William Pickens, branch organizer, arranged mass meetings to protest the ordinance and also started a branch in the city of Louisville. When the case reached the Supreme Court, the Baltimore branch filed an amicus curiae brief. The cities of Richmond and Baltimore filed amici curiae briefs in support of Louisville's position. Moorfield Storey and Clayton B. Blakey, lawyers for the plaintiff, argued before the Court:

> This ordinance [Louisville's] is an attempt to deprive the negro of the rights which belong to every citizen simply because white men consider him inferior by reason of his race and color. It was to protect him against precisely such consequences of race prejudice that the 14th Amendment was passed. . . . The crucial question is whether this ordinance deprives colored citizens of the enjoyment of all the civil rights that are enjoyed by white persons. . . . A plainer case of racial discrimination could not well be imagined.

In November 1917, the Supreme Court ruled that the Louisville ordinance violated the due process clause of the Fourteenth Amendment and denied persons the right "to acquire, enjoy and dispose" of property. Earlier, the Court had ruled that segregation was legal, but that it had its bounds, and the Louisville ordinance was outside those bounds. Basing its opinions on the Fourteenth Amendment and the accompanying statutes, the Court said,

The case presented does not deal with the attempt to prohibit the amalgamation of the races. The right which the ordinance annulled was the civil right of a white man to dispose of his property if he saw fit to do so to a person of color, and of a colored person to make such disposition to a white person. It is urged that this proposed segregation will promote the public peace, this aim cannot be accomplished by laws or ordinances which deny rights created or protected by the Federal Constitution.[16]

The NAACP rightly took credit for the victory, wrote to its branches telling them to play it up, and suggested that members of the Louisville chapter write a pamphlet on the story. The Association received a great deal of publicity and support from these cases. Unfortunately restrictive covenants in deeds were substituted for the residential ordinances, but these, too, would be fought.

In 1923, the Association argued *Moore v. Dempsey* before the Supreme Court. This case grew out of the violence following World War I and demonstrated that the system of tenancy and sharecropping that had afflicted Pink Franklin and Steve Greene a decade earlier had not changed. Black farmers in Philip County, Arkansas, having been organized by returning veterans, sought to get an accurate accounting from white landlords. The farmers, who were incorporated, had hired white lawyers from Little Rock. At a mass meeting called to discuss what the next step should be, the farmers were fired on by the deputy sheriff. The farmers returned the fire, killed the deputy, and wounded another person. The sheriff then deputized three hundred men, the governor of Arkansas mobilized five hundred federal troops, and for seven days they rounded up all the black farmers in the county, killing those who resisted. The official estimate of dead was twenty-five blacks, five whites. Walter White, investigating for the Association, said the number of blacks was more like two hundred.

The white landlords then "selected" for trial "good" blacks, those who had condemned the organizers and who agreed to work without pay for specified lengths of time for certain farmers; these blacks were freed. The others were put on trial for murder. Seventy-nine were indicted by an all-white grand jury and tried before an all-white jury. The first defendant did not see his lawyer until the trial, which lasted forty-five minutes. The jury deliberated five minutes before he was convicted. After a few more of these "trials," the rest of the blacks pleaded guilty to second-degree murder, which meant life in prison as opposed to first-degree murder and the death penalty. The cases were appealed by the NAACP.

Walter White reported this for the Association and the *Chicago Daily News*. His articles stirred the whole country. The Association received $50,000 in donations before the case went to the Supreme Court. Announcing for a divided Court, Justice Oliver Wendell Holmes said that everyone involved had been ruled by "public passion" and that the state courts should have reversed the lower court because the men had not had due process. Citing an earlier precedent Holmes declared:

> if in fact a trial is dominated by a mob, so that there is an actual interference with the course of justice, there is a departure from due process of law; and that if the state, supplying no corrective process, carries into execution a judgment of death or imprisonment based upon a verdict thus produced by mob domination, the state deprives that accused of his life or liberty without due process of law.[17]

The men were released by Arkansas. The NAACP had won a great victory. It had attacked another instance of mob violence, publicized the horror of the tenancy/sharecropping system, gained members and financial support, and found a potent propagandist in its assistant secretary.[18]

The next case before the Supreme Court in which the Association was involved was *Corrigan v. Bulkley*.[19] This case dealt with a restrictive covenant signed by a group of whites in Washington, D.C. One of the signers, Mrs. Corrigan, decided to sell her property to a black doctor, breaking her covenant. Mr. Bulkley, one of the co-signers of the covenant, sued Mrs. Corrigan. The NAACP in its arguments for the doctor before the Taft court said that the covenant denied the civil rights of the would-be owner and hence was more important than the property rights of the covenant signers. The Court disagreed in a unanimous decision. In the first major defeat of the Association before the Supreme Court, the progress made in *Buchanan v. Warley* was halted.

The Association had two cases before the Supreme Court in 1927: *Nixon v. Herndon,* involving the white primary; and *Harmon v. Taylor,* involving residential segregation by ordinance. In *Nixon v. Herndon,* Texas, relying upon an earlier Court case which said that primaries were not part of the election process, passed a law which said: "In no event shall a Negro be eligible to participate in a Democratic primary election in the State of Texas." The Association, through Arthur B. Spingarn and Fred Knollenberg, argued the case for Dr. A. L. Nixon on the basis of the Fifteenth Amendment. Through a bit of legal gymnastics, the Court decided the issue in Nixon's favor based on the Fourteenth Amendment's equal protection clause and ruled that race could not be used by the state to deny the vote to blacks. Justice Holmes delivered the opinion of the court,

> The statute of Texas, in the teeth of the prohibitions referred to [in the 14th Amendment], assumes to forbid negroes to take part in a primary election . . . discriminating against them by the distinction of color alone. States may do a good deal of classifying that is difficult to believe rational, but there are limits, and it is too clear for extended argument that color cannot be made the basis of a statutory classification.[20]

So Texas turned over the primary election qualification to the *party*'s executive committee. The Democratic party, not the state, then passed a resolution restricting primary voting to white Democrats, a Pyrrhic victory for the Association much like the *Buchanan v. Warley* case. Another residential segregation ordinance case was brought in 1927 by the Association. It involved a New Orleans ordinance, which read in part that "a member of one race might occupy property in areas zoned for another only if a majority of the residents consented." In *Harmon v. Taylor,* the Court agreed with the Association ruling that such segregation was illegal and based its decision on *Buchanan.*[21]

A final case that was entered but still pending at the time of the Parker fight was the *City of Richmond v. Deans.* Judge Parker ruled on the case in January 1930, from the Fourth Circuit Court of Appeals. Richmond had attempted residential segregation by passing an ordinance supposedly in support of Virginia's prohibition of intermarriage, which said that "no one might purchase or lease in a block where most of the residents belonged to a race into which the would-be dweller could not legally marry." Judge Parker, relying upon the *Buchanan v. Warley* decision, ruled the law unconstitutional.[22] On May 17, 1930, the United States Supreme Court agreed with Parker's ruling, basing its decision on *Buchanan v. Warley* and *Harmon v. Taylor.*[23]

The publicity that the Association received for its efforts provided it with another victory by showing that some progress in extending civil rights for black people and others could be attained through the courts. Hence, two ends could be met through one action—righting a wrong and publicizing the organization. For an organization that was perennially on the verge of bankruptcy, the publicity garnered by these cases was a valuable asset in fund raising and membership drives. The strategies and actions taken by the Association in its anti-lynching campaign and in the court cases—the newspaper publicity, the mass meetings, the branch publicity efforts, the investigations and legal challenges—all let black people know that the NAACP was working for them. In future years, the Association received a great deal of criticism for its "tactics," especially its publicity efforts. Critics later said that the publicity efforts of the Association appeared to aggrandize the Association more than it highlighted the injustice that was targeted for correction. At times, one wonders which came first, the perpetuation of the organization or the righting of a wrong. However, the history of black people in America and the history of the NAACP showed that without the continuation of the Association, many of the injustices inflicted upon black America would not have been righted. A people and an organization without financial resources and without power must use the tools available to them. For the NAACP, publicity and mass protest have proved to be effective tools, as demonstrated by the Parker fight.

2.

"THE NAACP COMES OF AGE"

The Defeat of Judge Parker

Given the history of the Association and the problems it faced, the success of its legal efforts was of paramount importance. As a result, any change on the Supreme Court bench was of vital interest to the NAACP leadership. On March 8, 1930, Associate Justice of the United States Supreme Court Edward Terry Sanford died. The Association was very concerned about his replacement. Acting Secretary Walter White wrote Elliot Thurston, a Washington bureau correspondent for the *New York World*, to inquire about a *World* story reporting that Senator Walter George (D-Georgia) was in line for the nomination.[1] White indicated to Thurston that George was unacceptable to the NAACP because of statements he had made concerning the Fourteenth and Fifteenth Amendments and their applicability to black rights. White did not want to waste resources attacking George if President Hoover was not serious about nominating him. James A. Cobb, a prominent black Republican and judge on the municipal court in Washington, D.C., received a similar letter from White a few days later, with an additional name which was then being floated—Harry W. Anderson, a lily-white Republican from Virginia. Thurston replied to White with an assessment of several possible candidates, including Judge Parker, who Thurston believed was too young to receive the appointment.[2] But the two most prominent names then being mentioned for the nomination were clearly anti-black southerners. Whoever received the nomination would certainly come under NAACP scrutiny.

Actually, neither George nor Anderson appeared on the first list of men considered for the associate justice position. Among the more notable personages who at least had biographies prepared for the president's consideration were the Honorable Benjamin Nathan Cardozo, associate judge, New York Court of Appeals; the Honorable Learned Hand, judge, U.S. Circuit Court, Second Circuit; the Honorable Owen J. Roberts, prominent corporate lawyer from Philadelphia; and Newton D. Baker, former mayor of Cleveland and secretary of war under Woodrow Wilson. The list of names included Republicans and Democrats from all sections of the country, although there was very strong pressure that Sanford, a southerner, be replaced by a southerner. The person selected by President Hoover and nominated to the Supreme Court was John J. Parker, judge of U.S. Circuit Court, Fourth Circuit.[3]

This was not the first time Parker had been considered for an appointment by the Hoover administration. In early February 1929, Hoover asked Mabel Walker Willebrandt, an assistant attorney general, to give her assessment of five men he was considering for attorney general. After giving her assessment of the list provided by the president, Willebrandt on her own suggested Judge Parker. She noted that Parker was young, that he had been appointed to a judgeship by President Coolidge, and, very important to Willebrandt, that "he represents the new South." Willebrandt also mentioned that Parker "has the high endorsement of Justice Stone."[4] However, the memo prepared by Associate Justice Harlan Fiske Stone for Hoover's consideration was much more tempered. Stone noted that the Parker appointment to the circuit bench had been a "surprise" but that Parker's work had been reviewed favorably. Stone then went on to write:

> I should say that he does not possess the intellectual acuteness or range of legal knowledge of the present Solicitor General for example. His political experience and contacts might favor approaches that could be well dispensed with in the public service. . . . My doubt would be as to his organizing and administrative capacity and whether he would have that suc-

cess of judgment and keenness of perception which would save him from having things put over him.[5]

He did not receive the appointment as attorney general.

Given Justice Stone's concerns and Parker's age (forty-five in 1930) and lack of experience (only five years as a circuit judge by 1930), why had President Hoover nominated him to the highest court of the land? A hint of an answer may be found in the biography prepared on Parker for President Hoover in conjunction with the Supreme Court nomination. The biography in part reads: "In 1920 [Parker] was nominee of the Republican Party for Governor of North Carolina, receiving 230,000 votes, which was 63,000 votes more than any candidate for Governor of either party had ever received prior to that time."[6] Although Parker failed to win the governorship, the Republican party viewed him as a valuable component in its plans to build a lily-white party in the South to challenge the lily-white Democrats.

Parker was born into a Democratic family, but the Republican party that he joined in 1908 had undergone many changes from its pre–Civil War inception. After Reconstruction, the GOP had virtually abandoned blacks and their struggle for civil rights, although the black vote remained wedded to the party. The abandonment was accentuated during the Taft presidency with the attempt to build an effective lily-white party in the South. Lily-white Republicans received appointments in Republican administrations of the period and "blacks and tans" were ousted from national, state, and local organizations. Republican legislators either actively supported or benignly looked on as southern Democrats placed their prejudices into law.[7]

President Hoover followed his lily-white predecessors in his 1928 preconvention moves. His general campaign strategy with its "southern emphasis" was successful in attracting some southern whites to the Republican party. Indeed, Hoover, as it has been argued, saw lily-white Republicans as the vanguard to the creation of the New South.[8] In this regard no finer example of the "New South" could probably have been found than Parker.

John Johnston Parker was born in 1885 in Monroe, North Carolina. He attended the University of North Carolina, gradu-

ating with an A.B. in 1907 and a L.L.B. in 1908. He started
his practice in Greensboro, where he offered his political services to the Democratic party. They refused his offer and he
apparently felt that there was more opportunity for him in
the Republican party, which he joined that year. His law practice
grew, as did his political ambition. The same year, he became
secretary of the Republican Campaign Committee for his district; in 1910, he ran unsuccessfully for Congress; in 1916, he
made an unsuccessful bid for the attorney general's office; and
in 1920, he was unsuccessful in his attempt to become the
first Republican governor since Reconstruction. His work for
the Republican party did not go unrecognized. In 1923, he
was appointed special assistant to the attorney general of the
United States; in 1924, he was elected a member of the Republican National Committee; and in 1925, President Calvin Coolidge
nominated him and the Senate confirmed him to the U.S. Court
of Appeals for the Fourth Circuit. The ultimate reward for Parker
was his nomination by Hoover to the Supreme Court.[9]

An examination of Parker's 1920 governor's campaign con-
firms that he belonged to Hoover's New South, lily-white elite.
The situation of the Republican party in North Carolina mir-
rored its situation throughout the South; it simply could not
break the near-stranglehold the lily-white Democrats had on
local and state politics. There was a brief break in Democratic
dominance in North Carolina, revolving around the Fusionist
movement begun in 1892. During that time Republicans (still
receiving black support) and Populists (also receiving black support) joined together to run candidates on the state and local
level. The Fusionists had some minor successes, particularly
on the local level, in electing Republicans and even a few blacks.
However, white suprematists within the Republican party opposed the movement because they believed the party could
never attain a majority without middle-class, white support,
and having blacks in the party would effectively block this.
While the Fusionists argued among themselves, the Democrats
regained control and continued to red-shirt Fusionists and any
Republican candidate who had a chance of winning. The Democrats also passed new election laws and a "grandfather clause"
in 1901 to ensure that black political participation would not
interfere with their party's dominance. At this point the Repub-

lican party abandoned all attempts to elicit black support and tried to out-lily-white the Democrats.[10]

Unfortunately for Parker, in his first contest for public office in 1910, his Democratic opponent red-shirted him, and what was considered a fairly progressive campaign went down to defeat. In 1916, when he ran for the attorney general's office, Parker's call for election reforms, more funding for public education, taxes for social services, and agricultural reform could not overcome his party's previous association with blacks. When Parker ran for governor in 1920, he wanted his campaign to succeed or fail on its own merits, not on the charge of black support. In this race he was not going to be out-lily-whited. He campaigned throughout North Carolina, denying that he had black support and supporting the lily-white movement within his party, which advocated the disfranchisement of blacks.

Parker's 1920 governor's campaign demonstrated that he was indeed a New South progressive. He called for women's suffrage, strong support for public education, industrial development, safeguards for labor, a state income tax, and better public roads. However, on the issue of race, he was loyal to his background, his region, and his party. In a speech delivered at his alma mater, Parker said:

> But what of the Negro question. Let me say this that I believe in a square deal for the Negro. . . . Experience has demonstrated that the participation of the Negro in the political life of the South is harmful to him and to the community, and is a fruitful source of that racial prejudice which works to his injury. As a class he has learned this lesson. He no longer desires to participate in politics. The Republican party of North Carolina does not desire him to participate in the politics of the state.[11]

Throughout the campaign Parker gave this speech and others similar to it to prove that he was part of the lily-white movement. In 1930, these credentials would help him secure Hoover's Supreme Court nomination, but they would also serve as the basis for the NAACP's objection to him.

After Parker's nomination was announced on March 21, Walter White investigated the nominee, as the Association had done with other nominees for the Court and other high federal appointments. As before, White contacted the various NAACP branches and "friends" around the country to see if anything was known of the nominees. Initially, little information could be gathered about Parker. However, on March 24, "reliable correspondents" sent the national office of the Association a clipping, dated April 19, 1920, from the *Greensboro Daily News*.[12] The article quoted a campaign speech Parker made, in which he said:

> The Republican party in North Carolina has accepted the amendment (of 1901, designed to keep the Negro from exercising of his right to the ballot) [parenthetical statement NAACP's] in that spirit in which it was passed and the Negro has so accepted it. I have attended every State Convention since 1908 and I have never seen a Negro delegate in any convention that I have attended. . . . I say it deliberately, there is no more dangerous or contemptible enemy of the state than men who for personal or political advantage will attempt to kindle the flame of racial prejudice. . . . The participation of the Negro in politics is a source of evil and danger to both races and is not desired by the wise men in either race or by the Republican party in North Carolina.[13]

The "reliable correspondent" was Dr. A. M. Riveria of the North Carolina Mutual Life Insurance Company and NAACP branch member. Dr. Riveria sent White the background information about Parker but insisted that White not reveal his name.[14] Statements like those quoted above were not atypical for southern politicians, yet for an organization that based its program for the advancement of black people on a legal strategy, such a person was clearly unacceptable on the Supreme Court.

To see if Parker still held such views, White telegraphed the judge on March 26, requesting a confirmation or denial of the newspaper article. Although the telegram was delivered (Western Union notified the national office), no response was ever received.[15] On March 28, the national office sent letters to 177 branches, in selected states, asking them to contact their senators requesting that the nomination be rejected. The same day, the NAACP sent letters directly to the senators with the same request.[16] The NAACP campaign to defeat the Parker nomination was in motion.

The fight to defeat Judge Parker and its immediate aftermath form an important chapter in the history of the Association. Not only was a "racist" judge kept from the Supreme Court, but the Association's campaign became a tool for raising money and memberships in the face of Depression-era retrenchment. In addition, the Parker fight provided members of the NAACP with practical leadership training on the national, state, and local levels in grass-roots politics and activism. This experience served the organization well in its future ventures, and it bolstered race consciousness and pride at a time when both had sunk low because of adverse economic conditions and heightened racism.

The campaign to defeat the Parker nomination was initially fought in the Senate. Acting Secretary White had sent a letter to Senator George Norris (R-Nebraska), chairman of the Senate Judiciary Committee, lodging the NAACP's objections to Parker and requesting an appearance before the committee. White was informed that the Parker nomination was before a subcommittee of the Judiciary Committee, and arrangements were made for him to appear on April 5.[17]

Concurrently, the NAACP wrote President Hoover, citing the Association's objections and requesting that he withdraw the nomination, giving as a precedent President Taft's withdrawal of a judicial nomination in 1912 because of the nominee's anti-Negro stands. Hoover refused.[18]

White then appeared before the subcommittee on April 5, and wrote in his secretary's report for the April meeting of the Association's board of directors that

> the Acting Secretary was received with courtesy by the committee and it was the general impression . . . that the Association's protest was amply justified and that it would have a salutary effect . . . upon the case of Judge Parker.[19]

White's later recollection of the hearing was less glowing. In his autobiography, he wrote that he and William Green, president of the American Federation of Labor, entered the hearing room at the same time. They had met on numerous occasions in the past, and yet Green "appeared conspicuously to avoid speaking lest senators on the committee, newspapermen, or spectators believe that we were fighting in a common battle. . . . I was not called upon until the very end of the hearing."[20] Writing in *Harper's* the following year, White toned down his assessment of the hearing, saying that "the spokesman [White] for the Negroes was heard only after all other protestants had been allowed to speak, and even then his statement aroused only mild interest."[21]

A look at the subcommittee testimony affirms this last assessment of senatorial attitude toward his testimony, but White was not the last witness to testify. The last witness was Mercer G. Johnson, director of the People's Legislative Service, who opposed Parker's nomination on the basis of his conservative interpretation of the constitution.[22] None of the witnesses, including Green, attempted to link their objections to White's and the NAACP's cause. Green had lodged an objection to Parker on the basis of his upholding of yellow-dog contracts. Yellow-dog contracts were instruments developed in the 1920s to ensure an open shop in the mines. Basically, the contracts, which had to be signed as a prerequisite for employment, declared that the signer was not a member of a union and that he agreed not to join a union while employed. The United Mine Workers had spent eight million dollars trying to break these contracts, but the federal courts (including Parker) had held them to be constitutional under the Hitchman Doctrine, which allowed courts to issue injunctions upholding the provision of the contract.[23]

During the hearing the senators carefully questioned White about the NAACP's objections to Parker. The subcommittee records show that Senator Lee Overman (D-North Carolina) questioned White most intensely. Overman insinuated that Dr. Moulton [Moton, Head of Tuskegee Institute] and Parker held the same position on black suffrage. In addition, Overman challenged White to produce evidence that any Negro had been blocked from voting in North Carolina, adding that Parker had even received black support in the governor's race in 1920. White could not produce such evidence at that time. Senator William Borah (R-Idaho), a Progressive, also asked probing questions of White. Borah wanted something more specific than the general accusations against Parker:

> *Senator Borah:*   Do you know anything in the career of Judge Parker to indicate that he is unfriendly of the Negro?

Mr. White:	Nothing except this statement (the newspaper article) here.
Senator Borah:	Except that statement you have there?
Mr. White:	This one statement.
Senator Borah:	Do you know of anything in his career that you have heard of, where he has been in any way unjust?
Mr. White:	Frankly, we never heard of him until he was nominated by President Hoover.[24]

White's impression on the subcommittee was not as strong as he described it to the Association's board of directors at their April meeting, and he recognized that the fight against Parker would take place on other ground.

Overman's allegation that Parker received Negro support had to be countered, and it soon was. According to White:

> Following publication in the press of the report of the hearing, the National Office received lengthy telegrams from North Carolina Negroes, . . . denying the truth of Senator Overman's statement and declaring that Judge Parker said in his campaign that he did not want Negro votes and that Judge Parker did not receive Negro votes.[25]

The national office telegraphed every branch of the NAACP and told them to urge senators to vote against Parker. Branches were also asked to contact other white and black organizations, such as churches, lodges, and fraternal organizations, for the purpose of protesting the Parker nomination. Perhaps the largest organization to lend its support was the National Association of Colored Women, which numbered over 250,000 members (by its own count).[26]

As the NAACP's campaign against Parker gained momentum, the Senate subcommittee did the expected, and on April 14, it approved Parker's nomination by a two-to-one vote. Senators Lee Overman and Felix Herbert (R-Rhode Island) had indicated their support for Parker even before the hearing. Senator William Borah voted against Parker on the yellow-dog contract issue. April 28 was set for hearings by the full judiciary committee.[27]

Judge Parker's supporters wasted no time in buttressing his cause, and White noted that "as the fight waxed bitter, virtually every trick of legislative maneuvering, fair, or foul, was utilized."[28] They first charged that he had never made the offensive campaign statements, a claim that was immediately refuted when the Association sent copies of the newspaper article to President Hoover, to every senator, and to every correspondent in Washington. Parker's supporters then charged that the clipping had been stolen (it had), but fortunately for the NAACP, the charge was never considered seriously. Parker's supporters went even further, and White wrote that "lobbyists with thick Southern accents buttonholed . . . [senators from the South] and, asking contemptuously whether they were going to bow to the dictation of a 'nigger' advancement society."[29]

Two Negro "leaders" from North Carolina, M. K. Tyson, president of the National Association of Negro Tailors, and Dr. J. E. Shephard, president of North Carolina College for Negroes, had written statements in support of Parker's nomination, and these received wide attention as the fight continued.[30] In addition to publicly supporting Parker, Shephard wrote to Overman giving Parker his endorsement, and he also wrote to Carl Murphy, the editor of the *Baltimore Afro-American*.[31] Shephard told Murphy, "I know his personal friendly attitude to my race and to me. I believe that if he is elevated to the Supreme Court Bench that the Negro will have no fairer or truer friend."[32] Shephard helped orchestrate a counter-campaign by asking "representative colored men" from several states to send endorsements of Parker to their senators.[33] While Shephard may have been moved by goodwill toward Parker, Tyson appeared to be motivated by both goodwill and monetary gain. Tyson wrote to Parker on March 28, giving his endorsement and then suggesting that he would take a delegation to Washington to lobby for Parker in the Senate; however, he would need $1,000 for this endeavor. Parker wrote back thanking him for his endorsement but politely turning down his offer to help.[34] On May 7, after offering his condolences for Parker's defeat and citing all the things he had done for Parker, Tyson wrote: "My actual expense has been $530.59. I suggest you send me a cashier's check covering my expenses which will not bear your name." Again, Parker politely refused.[35]

Support for Parker also came from one Negro newspaper, the *Topeka Plaindealer*. The news release from the Associated Negro Press, which announced the support, also mentioned that the *Plaindealer* had accepted a quarter-page advertisement for "The Birth of a Nation."[36] Parker's black supporters received harsh condemnation from the Negro press and black leaders.[37] Other black leaders, such as Dr. Moton of Tuskegee, whom President Hoover had appointed to the Haitian Investigation Committee, also received overtures from Parker supporters, but Moton, like most other blacks solicited by Parker's friends, would not support the judge.[38] The requests for support for Parker were being made so widely, or perhaps so desperately, that even Mary White Ovington, chairman of the board of directors of the NAACP, was telephoned to see if she supported Parker.[39]

Except for the few highly publicized defections, black leaders were solidly behind the NAACP effort. The Negro press was one of the most important backers of the Association. It was particularly useful in disseminating to a wider black audience information about the fight against Parker. Mrs. Beulah E. Young, vice-president of the Associated Negro Press, sent Hoover a telegram from all one hundred members of the press association demanding that Judge Parker's name be withdrawn. Throughout the fight, the Associated Negro Press sent weekly news releases to Negro newspapers around the country condemning Parker for his views and Hoover for nominating him, and giving the main credit for the fight to the NAACP.[40] A typical example of these news releases was one entitled "Parker Fight Shows Up Some Negro Friends," dated May 7, 1930. According to the news release:

> The well-organized and industrious campaign against the confirmation of Parker conducted by the National Association for the Advancement of Colored People under the personal leadership of Walter F. White has put the backs of a large number of United States Senators to the wall. . . .

It claimed that "the administration forces are aware that without the battle waged by the NAACP, the labor people could have been steamrollered."[41] The news articles in the Negro press implied that the NAACP had been the only effective force to combat and ultimately defeat Parker.

By April 21, what had seemed a sure thing to Parker's supporters was seriously in doubt; his friends in Congress were even willing to take the unprecedented step of having him testify in person.[42] However, the judiciary committee defeated the proposal, ten to six, and reported his nomination out of committee, adversely, by the same vote. The adverse vote was due to a multitude of reasons, including objections from the NAACP and Democrats.[43]

Parker's willingness to take the extraordinary step of personally testifying was characteristic of his behavior throughout the confirmation battle. From March 10 to May 7, Parker was actively engaged in the political skirmishes that took place in the United States Senate. This behavior, for 1930, was questionable in terms of propriety and demonstrated Parker's eagerness to ascend to the Supreme Court bench. If the Senate had been fully aware of Parker's behind-the-scenes activities, one can only wonder if another issue might not have been added to the debate. For example, Parker consulted Charles Jonas, a member of the Republican National Committee from North Carolina, and Thomas W. Davis, a prominent attorney from North Carolina, on an almost daily basis on tactics and strategies to be employed. Parker supplied his two operatives with names of people to be contacted and even the names of friends of friends to be contacted on his behalf. The correspondence and telephone calls between Parker, Jonas, and Davis indicate a major effort for his confirmation. In addition, Parker wrote a defense of his position on the labor and race issue to be distributed to his supporters inside and outside of the Senate. Besides Jonas and Davis, Parker had a myriad of supporters who kept him informed of their efforts for his success. One interesting point about this voluminous correspondence was that by mid-April the focus of the lobbying shifted from defending Parker on the labor issue to increasingly defending him on the race issue. It should also be noted that David Blair, another prominent North Carolina Republican, and Jonas made an informal count and predicted that Parker would be easily confirmed in his nomination—fifty-six for, sixteen to twenty-four opposed, the rest undecided.[44] Parker received two letters in mid-April, both from supporters advising him of their work. In one, Senator Robinson Smith (D-South Carolina), who was ill and would not be present for any votes, was urged to pair his vote with an anti-Parker senator who would also not be present. Parker's correspondent wrote, "We impressed on him the seriousness of the attack that is being made on you and especially by the Negro opposition. . . ."[45] Another operative had just received a supportive letter from Senator Simeon Fess (R-Ohio) and wrote, "I am particularly pleased with his attitude inasmuch as Ohio is one of the states where the Negro is in evidence in sufficient numbers to be reckoned with politically."[46] A copy of an anti-Parker letter from Senator A. H. Vandenburg (R-Michigan) was forwarded to Parker, in which Vandenburg indicated that "the thing that disturbs me is the following quotation"; he then cited part of Parker's 1920 speech and ended the letter by questioning whether Parker could shake off all of his "predilections" and by stating that he believed that "colored citizens have a right to be suspicious."[47] This is not to say that all of Parker's correspondence in the final two weeks involved the race issue; it did not. His correspondence reflected a shift from concern over the labor issue to a greater concern over the damage that the race issue might inflict.

Debate by the entire Senate began on April 28. Senator Overman made a few supportive remarks for Parker; Borah followed with a stinging attack against Parker on the yellow-dog contract issue. Senator Fess supported Parker on the grounds that his detractors were "radicals," and Senator Wagner (D-New York) linked the yellow-dog issue with Parker's 1920 speech.

An upstate New York branch of the NAACP wrote Wagner on April 4 to state its objections to Parker, and the Senator may have based his comments partially on the branch letter.[48] Other senators were not encouraged to link the issues, because Seligman and White warned "that insistence upon any anti-Negro utterance of Parker" at the moment might alienate those southern senators who would otherwise vote against Parker.[49] From April 28 onward, the issues of race, labor, and conservatism were brought to the fore, and on Wednesday, May 7, the Parker nomination was defeated by a vote of forty-one to thirty-nine.[50]

The defeat of the nomination of Judge Parker was the NAACP's most successful national endeavor since its inception. The Association had carried on a national lobbying campaign, and with the assistance of other organizations, it had kept a "racist" judge from the Supreme Court bench. Parker's defeat

in the Senate also set back Hoover's plans for creating a lily-
white Republican party in the South, and the entire lobbying
effort politicized black people as few events before ever had.
For the NAACP, however, the greatest accomplishment of the
fight was the widespread publicity and financial support the
organization received. The Great Depression had an adverse
effect on self-help and welfare organizations, and for black
groups the effects were truly disastrous, because the Depression
started earlier and became more severe for blacks than for the
general population. These deteriorating conditions coupled
with black criticism of the NAACP meant some means had
to be found to generate positive interest, membership, and
funds; for the NAACP the solution was the Parker case.
Whether or not Walter White and the NAACP had all three
goals in mind when they started the campaign is unclear, but
the methods and the results suggest that after the campaign
started, such institutional objectives became a primary concern.[51]

As the campaign directed at the Senate proceeded, the Association carried its message to the nation's black population
through its national office, the organization's field workers, and
the black press. The black rank and file, however, would not
be the ones who would vote on Parker, and there is little evidence to suggest that senators with black constituencies initially
took black protest seriously. But in taking the campaign to the
masses, the NAACP demonstrated, as never before, that it was
working for black people and deserved their moral and financial
support.

While individuals such as Arthur B. Spingarn (an early legal
counsel and prominent member of the executive committee
of the NAACP) and W. E. B. Du Bois addressed mass rallies
and received widespread news coverage, the real work of the
campaign was carried out by White, Robert Bagnall, William
Pickens, and Daisy Lampkin.[52]

Between April 5 and April 30, in addition to carrying out
his other duties as acting secretary, Walter White addressed
protest and branch meetings in New York, Chicago, Detroit,
and Cleveland against the Parker nomination, gaining contributions, memberships and telegrams to senators, along with growing appreciation of the work of the organization. Robert Bagnall

addressed meetings in Pittsburgh, Akron, Chicago, St. Louis, and Kansas City with the same results. William Pickens, on vacation in California during part of this time, centered his activities there.

The work of Regional Secretary Daisy Lampkin, who had only started in her temporary position in February 1930, deserves special mention. Director of Branches Bagnall praised her work as she crisscrossed the Midwest working for the organization and the defeat of Parker.[53] An example of her impact may be found in Bagnall's report for the June board of director's meeting, where he described her work:

> Mrs. Lampkin has been specializing in drives and organizational work. Under her leadership this year the Pittsburgh Branch obtained more than seven hundred and fifty members. She recently conducted a drive in Indianapolis, where the Branch has been nearly moribund for some time, raising more than eight hundred dollars. As a result of her efforts in Indianapolis, the Branch will meet apportionment in full for the first time in four years. Mrs. Lampkin has now attacked the most difficult of all Branches, Baltimore, and indications are that she will be successful in securing more than a thousand members [she did].[54]

During all of this activity, the correspondence among these NAACP workers shows their awareness of the organizational impact of their campaign. In a letter from Daisy Lampkin to Robert Bagnall, on April 17, Mrs. Lampkin, although "praying that we will win this fight," observed that "even if we don't there has been nothing that has attracted such wide attention." She concluded that "it is bound to help us."[55] A week later she wrote almost the same letter to the acting executive secretary.[56]

On May 2, Walter White emphasized the dual nature of the campaign when he wrote to Bagnall, Pickens, and Lampkin that

> letters of commendation of the Association for its fight against Parker are pouring into the office and indicate a golden opportunity to increase the membership of the Association. We must translate this enthusiasm for the Association into larger membership and greater financial support. Never has the

Association had the widespread approval which it now has
and it is up to us to utilize the occasion for increasing financial
support of the Association.[57]

The NAACP victory in the fight served to boost the organization, as revealed in a letter from Lampkin to White on May
9. After congratulating White for his "fine leadership," she
told him, "Indianapolis is on its toes in this drive and we
are using the Parker victory as a selling point."[58]

Not only the field workers but the black media believed that
the fight against Parker demanded a response of black support
for the Association. An article in the *Amsterdam News* stated:

The organizing of Negro opposition and the forcing of the
Negro question to the front demonstrates again the value
of such an organization as the National Association for the
Advancement of Colored People. . . . It has succeeded in
arousing the greatest activity on behalf of the Negro that
has been seen for years. The Association needs and should
have the unstinting support of every Negro in the country.[59]

Herbert J. Seligman was even more direct about the support
that the Parker fight could gain for the organization. Writing
in the June 1930, issue of *The Crisis*, Seligman observed that

The National Office mainly concerned with this fight from
the beginning disregarded matters of expense. They went
ahead . . . relying upon colored people . . . to rally to them
and help them to meet expenses. . . . Colored and liberal
white people have had a chance now to see what . . . the
Association can do in a critical situation. It is up to them
to help pay the bills.[60]

The NAACP's success in the Parker fight became its rallying
cry for organizational support in the 1930s.[61]

The defeat of Judge Parker's nomination to the Court represented the efforts of the Association and other groups, such
as the AFL, liberals, and Democrats. In the process, NAACP
leaders made it known that black people, represented by the
Association, had a distinct interest in anyone nominated to
sit on the Court, and that they would organize to fight anti-black
nominees. The Negro press, led by the Associated Negro Press,
gave the Association unstinting support. The fight even gar-

nered respect from the initially skeptical and, in some cases, openly hostile white press.[62] All of this helped sustain the organization through the rough years of the Great Depression. Membership figures are not available, but one indication of growing support for the organization is the record of branch contributions. In 1929, the branches remitted $40,797.15 to the national office. In 1930, the first full year of the Depression, the branches sent in $35,492.10. The following year, in response to the electoral campaigns, branch contributions were up to $39,334.91, but by 1932 branch contributions had dropped back to $20,226.89. Without a major campaign to secure nationwide publicity and support, the Association could have easily gone the way of many other organizations and businesses during this time.[63]

The pride, self-esteem, and race consciousness black people felt, along with the confidence the Association gained, cannot be measured, but they appear to have been increased by the fight. After the Parker vote, Heywood Broun, a white liberal intellectual, claimed in *The Crisis* that "the fight against the confirmation of Judge Parker for the Supreme Court was one of the most useful incidents which has ever occurred to give the American Negro a consciousness of his voting power."[64] The Parker fight marked the height of the black insurgency movement against the Republicans, and black Americans began to see the Democrats as offering a viable alternative to the lily-white party of Hoover.[65]

It may have exaggerated the Association's role, but the best summary of the effects of the Parker fight was given by William H. Hastie, a highly respected, long-time civil rights lawyer later to be appointed federal judge and governor of the Virgin Islands. In an article printed in *The Crisis* in 1939, entitled "A Look at the NAACP," Hastie provided a fitting tribute to the organization's efforts:

> Through the agency of this Association, America was made to realize that, after a long lapse following the Reconstruction, the Negro again had become a powerful and an important figure in national politics. The dramatic occasion for that demonstration was the battle in the United States Senate against the confirmation of Judge John J. Parker. . . . That victory

and the subsequent defeat of Senators who had voted to confirm the Parker nomination probably impressed the nation more than any other thing accomplished by the American Negro during the 20th century. For years to come it will remain fresh and persuasive in the minds of politicians and all aspirants to Federal Office.[66]

With the Parker fight behind it, the NAACP could and did enter into the mainstream of national protest organizations. Whether or not the Association was aware of the overall impact of this case, one cannot but think it at least had an inkling when the national office chose as the motto for the twenty-first annual convention in 1930, "The NAACP Comes of Age."[67] The organization had set out clear objectives, effectively conveyed them to the masses, marshaled its resources, and won a significant victory, not only in new members and financial support but also in respect from blacks and whites throughout the country.

3.

THE PARKER FIGHT

Precursor to the New Deal Coalition and the Black Insurgency Movement

The defeat of the Parker nomination meant that from 1930 onward blacks and some whites recognized the NAACP as the leading civil rights organization in the United States. The Parker fight did more than just catapult the NAACP into the spotlight. The struggle over Parker's confirmation brought about an awareness of the importance of the black electorate, something that had been ignored since the end of Reconstruction. The issue of race was a crucial factor in the defeat of the Parker nomination. The forces which coalesced to defeat the nomination were the same forces that would later make up the New Deal coalition, and blacks played a prominent role in both.

There are several reasons why historians in general have not given the race issue or the NAACP much credit for the defeat of the nomination.[1] One is the historiography itself. Few historians have studied the political role of black people and the NAACP, particularly between the time of the "final capitulation to racism" in the 1890s and the formal entry of black people into the New Deal coalition. Weighted against the historiography of the labor movement during the same period, the few studies devoted to blacks show that historians have relied on labor's view of the story, in which an aroused AFL struck out at the injunctions and yellow-dog contracts. In addition, historians have been aware of how small and weakened the NAACP had become by 1930. The organization was never large, certainly not in terms of the numbers of the AFL. The NAACP in its pre-1930 phase had not gained much publicity, because it sought to redress grievances in the courts and not in the streets. The only previous fully coordinated lobbying campaign had been the unsuccessful attempt at the passage of the Dyer Anti-Lynching Bill.[2]

More important has been the underestimation of the black insurgency movement that was under way. The Great Migration from the rural South to northern cities during and after World War I was filled with politically liberating influences. A number of factors politicized black people: the outspokenness of Marcus Garvey, A. Phillip Randolph, and others on the issues of civil rights and black consciousness; the persistence of lynchings; the election of Oscar de Priest to Congress; the growth and virulence of the lily-white Republican in the 1920s in the South; and the legal lobbying activities of the NAACP. All of these were covered by the growing and strident black press led by the *Chicago Defender,* the *Pittsburgh Courier,* the *Baltimore Afro-American,* and the Associated Negro Press. Black people were becoming active players, not just potential voters waiting to be seduced into the New Deal coalition.

Senators in states with sizeable and growing black electorates were well aware of black political stirrings. A fuller assessment of the Senate debate on the Parker nomination shows that the issue of race along with the labor issue and Parker's conservatism all contributed to his defeat.

Even before the full debate began, senators started entering materials in the *Congressional Record* to buttress their positions once they took the floor. As early as April 7, Robert Wagner had entered Parker's Circuit Court opinion in the case of *UMW v. Red Jacket Consolidated Coal & Coke,* as well as *Interborough Rapid Transit v. Green et al.* from the Supreme Court of New York. The Red Jacket case grew out of an attempt by the United Mine Workers to organize mines in Mingo County, Virginia, in 1923. The coal operators went to court to seek injunctions against the union. Temporary injunctions were granted. The United Mine Workers appealed to the Fourth Circuit Court. Parker enjoined the union from unlawful organizing activities and upheld the companies' use of the yellow-dog contract based on Supreme Court rulings in *Hitchman Coal & Coke Co. v. Mitchell*, which Parker noted,

> enjoined interference with the contract by means of peaceful persuasion. . . . To make a speech or to circulate an argument under ordinary circumstances dwelling upon the advantages of union membership is one thing. To approach a company's employees working under a contract not to join the union while remaining in the company's service . . . is [a] very difficult thing . . . and what was said in the Hitchman case with respect to this matter is conclusive of the point involved here.

Judge Parker had clearly been following the precedents established by the Supreme Court. However, in the *Interborough Rapid Transit* case, given the same questions of the union's right to organize workers who had signed yellow-dog contracts, the New York court found that, while acknowledging *Hitchman*,

> the defendants [William Green and the AFL] have the right to induce the plaintiff's employees to join the amalgamated association, though that may involve termination of their employment. . . . The defendants are acting for themselves or the amalgamated association and in taking lawful action to advance the interest of the members of that union they are under no affirmative duty of protecting the privileges or even the rights of the plaintiff.[3]

Ruling on the same issues, the New York courts disagreed with the findings of Parker's ruling and did not feel compelled by Supreme Court precedent, a point that would come up in the debate. On April 14, Lee Overman entered an editorial from the *Atlanta Constitution* supporting Parker on the yellow-dog contract decision, saying that he was only following Supreme Court precedent and that "qualified Negro voters" in North Carolina were not upset with Parker's views on race: "It is the hell-raising political vampires of New York and Boston who are fighting the Parker nomination, purely on color-line contentions."[4] On the eighteenth of April, George Norris entered a long editorial from the *Washington Daily News* concerning injured workers, workmen's compensation, and employer's liability laws, and emphasizing how difficult it had been to achieve these protections. The editorial stated that if Parker were confirmed, another anti-labor judge would be added to the court, and who knew what might happen to hard-won labor laws? On the same day, Cole Blease (D-South Carolina), a Parker supporter, had entered a letter to President Hoover from the Society of Friends' Committee on Race Relations, dated April 17, expressing their opposition to Parker. Other items entered by Overman defending Parker on the labor and race issues indicated the direction the debate would take.[5]

The first speaker in the floor debate on April 28 was Overman. As senior senator from the home state of the nominee and as a member of the pro-Parker minority on the judiciary committee, Overman presented the case for the nominee. He had entered into the record an open letter he had received from Parker defending himself on the labor issue (saying that he had only followed Supreme Court precedent) and on the race issue (saying that he had not wanted race to be an issue in the 1920 election). Overman stressed Parker's education and experience and noted that "he [Parker] has never shown any feelings against the colored man that anybody can cite except in one speech—a political speech. . . . A man ought not to be held responsible for what he said in a political speech."[6] He then attempted to retire to the sidelines to allow Republican party regulars to carry the full brunt of the debate. But Hugo Black (D-Alabama) questioned Parker's conduct as special assistant to U.S. Attorney General William Dougherty in the war profiteering cases (cases which had initially brought Parker to public attention, helping him secure his circuit court appointment). Black implied that Parker had been less than honorable in his handling of the case, and that he possibly even withheld evidence that would have helped prove the defendants' innocence. Overman said that these charges were untrue and that he could prove it; he did. Letters of support for Parker from blacks were also entered into the record, as were favorable editorials stating that opposition to Parker was "an attack upon the fundamentals of government." Another editorial charged that if Parker were rejected it would be because senators who were up for reelection, regardless of party, had been frightened by the "bogey of the colored vote." Another editorial said that "the attack upon Judge Parker is in reality an attack upon the

Supreme Court. . . . The purpose . . . is to terrorize all Federal judges so that they will not dare to perform their duty in issuing injunctions in labor disputes."[7]

Next to speak was Senator William Borah (R-Idaho), a progressive and the lone dissenter on the judiciary subcommittee. He launched a strong attack against Parker on the yellow-dog issue. In rebuttal to Parker's supporters' claims that Parker had ruled in favor of the yellow-dog contract only because the Supreme Court had previously decided on the issue, Borah pointed out that Judge Benjamin Cardozo of the New York Court of Appeals and the Supreme Court of Kansas had both rejected the legality of the yellow-dog contract. In the U.S. Supreme Court *Hitchman* case, Brandeis, Holmes, and Clark had dissented from the majority in attempting to disallow yellow-dog contracts and injunctions. There was clear precedent for disagreeing with the Court if Parker wanted to see it. Borah's speech, which lasted for over an hour on Monday, had to be carried over until Tuesday so that the Senate could conduct other business.[8]

The labor issue that centered on the yellow-dog contract and the injunction issue was only the tip of the iceberg in terms of labor's sentiments. Hoover's nomination of Parker came after a decade of action against unions. In the decade from 1920 to 1930, 921 injunctions were issued. This was half the number of injunctions issued in the previous fifty-year period from 1880 to 1930. Moreover, there were very few strikes in the 1920s, yet the injunction remedy was gaining popularity. Employers used the injunction as their most frequent and most pronounced weapon, but organized labor was also under attack through damage suits against their unions, prosecution under the Sherman Antitrust Act, and criminal prosecutions against labor organizers and strikers.[9] Parker, with his adherence to stated Supreme Court policy, felt constrained to agree with these actions. By 1930, such a justice was no longer acceptable on the Supreme Court.

Borah concluded on Tuesday, the twenty-ninth. Others objecting to Parker's nomination included Senator Dill (D-Washington), who stressed Parker's lack of judicial independence. Dill argued that if Parker had been as swayed by the previous Supreme Court decision as his supporters indicated, then he could not be counted upon to decide cases before the Court on their own merits.[10]

Senator Gillette (R-Massachusetts) then took to the floor and defended Parker on the labor issue. He went on to the race question: "On that issue I differ absolutely from Judge Parker. . . . But I recognize that different environments have occasioned different opinions on that question." Gillette had devised a formula whereby he could support Parker on the labor issue, raise his objections about Parker's statement on Negroes in politics, and still be a good Republican; other senators also took this option.[11]

Touching upon this theme and raising others, Senator Robert Wagner took to the floor on the third day of debate and launched one of the more important attacks on Parker, quoting Chief Justice Hughes: "The Constitution is what the judges say it is. Past judges made the current constitution and current judges will make the future constitution, and this is the standard by which Parker or any nominee should be judged." Wagner then discussed the four problems he saw dividing the court. The first two were the questions of the limits of a state's police power and the state's power to tax to fund social welfare. The third problem was in the field of public utility regulation. And the fourth concerned industrial relations and what actions employees could take to secure their own economic interest. "The nature of the personnel of the Supreme Court," Wagner said, "will determine whether the area of permitted action shall be wide and free or narrowly restricted." He then attacked Parker directly on the yellow-dog issue, saying that no employer had ever sued an employee for failing to live up to the contract. It was just used as a pretext to secure an injunction against union organizing. Because Parker could not see this point, he did not deserve to be on the bench. Wagner then went on to link the labor and race issues.

> Mr. President, I see a deep and fundamental consistency between Judge Parker's views on labor relations and his reported attitude toward the colored people of the United States. He is obviously incapable of viewing with sympathy the aspirations of those who are aiming for a higher and better place in the world.[12]

It should be noted that the Senate had just concluded another Supreme Court nomination battle in February 1930. Upon the resignation of Chief Justice Howard Taft, President Hoover nominated Charles Evans Hughes, with Taft's blessing and recommendation, to the chief justice's seat. Hughes was respected, his qualifications were impeccable: he had served on the Court as an associate justice under Taft from 1910 to 1916, and had been secretary of state under Harding. Still Hughes's nomination ran into trouble. He was opposed by a coalition of Progressive members of the president's party and Democratic liberals; Norris, Borah, La Follette (R-Wisconsin), and Wheeler (D-Montana) were some of the more prominent members of this coalition.

The Hughes nomination had difficulty because some senators were already upset with Hoover's handling of the economic downturn; opposing the nomination was a way of attacking the president. Also, Hughes, after leaving the Court and following his unsuccessful bid for the presidency, had gone into corporate law, representing businesses and people of great wealth—the very people, some senators believed, who were responsible for the economic situation. But more important was the issue of his conservatism. For the Progressive Republicans and Democratic liberals, the Depression had confirmed the bankruptcy of the conservative decisions of the Court in the 1920s, and they felt (rightly so) that Hughes would not be a stimulus for change. As Norris put it, "No man in public life so exemplifies the influence of powerful combinations in the political and financial world as does Mr. Hughes."[13] The nomination was saved finally by the support of Wagner and Royal Copeland (D-New York), Hughes's home state senators; the vote was fifty-six to twenty-six; fourteen senators abstained.

Following Wagner in the debate was McKellar (D-Tennessee), who questioned Parker's abilities as a lawyer and judge. McKellar also felt that Parker's letter to Overman "fell far short of explaining either" (his "Red Jacket" opinion and his statement about colored people).[14] Then McKellar introduced the "Dixon letter."

The Dixon letter explicitly raised an issue that had been behind a great deal of the opposition to Parker but that had never before been articulated in the debate. The letter, from the Honorable Joseph M. Dixon, first assistant secretary of the interior, to the Honorable Walter H. Newton, secretary to Hoover, dated March 13, 1930, observed that North Carolina gave President Hoover a 65,000 majority in the 1920 presidential election. "In my judgment," wrote Dixon, "it carries more hope of future permanent alignment with the Republican Party than any other of the Southern states that broke from their political moorings last year."[15] Dixon was, of course, alluding to the attempt by the Republicans to create a lily-white southern party. Republicans had scored their most impressive success to date in the South, increasing their hope of creating a permanent shift in southern political allegiances.

Hoover's part in this strategy goes back to the primary election of 1928, in which he welcomed lily-white support, often at the expense of delegations that had "blacks and tans." In fact, the only black and tan delegations seated were those that had declared for him. His forces controlled the process through Mabel Walker Willebrandt, chair of the credentials committee for the 1928 convention. One of the most prominent and respected southern black Republicans to declare for Hoover before the election was Perry Howard of Mississippi. Howard, as head of Mississippi's blacks and tans, had been able to fight off an attempt by his own state party leaders to unseat him and his delegation. Immediately after the convention, Mrs. Willebrandt, who was also an assistant attorney general, indicted Howard, one of the few remaining black national committeemen, on charges of corruption and selling political patronage. Benjamin Davis, black national committeeman from Georgia, was indicted on the same charges. Davis, like Howard, had also endorsed Hoover before the convention. No white Republicans or Democrats were indicted. In the election, Hoover carried six southern states: Florida, Kentucky, North Carolina, Texas, Virginia, and West Virginia.[16]

Because of the embarrassment caused by the indictments of two of the most prominent black Republicans in the country, President Hoover was very slow about rewarding black patronage and stubbornly refused Robert Moton's advice that black Republicans had to be mollified soon with some appointments or he stood a chance of losing them. On February 5, 1930,

Moton wrote to Hoover with names of possible appointees. He suggested three possible candidates for the specialist in child welfare at the Bureau of Child Welfare. One of the names was Mrs. Daisy Lampkin, whom Moton described thus: "Mrs. Daisy Lampkin served during the Presidential Campaign as Director of Colored Women's Activities. . . . She is a prominent club woman and has had much experience as an organizer."[17] She was not appointed to the position, and three months later she became an organizer for the NAACP. It is interesting to reflect on what would have occurred had she received an appointment to the Bureau of Child Welfare.

On the other hand, opportunities to reward the lily-whites were promptly seized upon, and several lily-whites were appointed to prominent positions; hence the Parker nomination in 1930. Hoover had been so impressed with Parker that he had even considered him for the cabinet as attorney general. Parker's 1920 governor's statement was the epitome of the lily-white strategy.

For the Democratic party, their fall from national power had been the result of a number of factors, principally the break-up of the tenuous Wilson coalition of 1916. This coalition consisted of Progressives, urban ethnic groups, labor, and the important Bryanite agrarian vote. The Democratic party had hoped this would be a permanent realignment, providing support for tough controls on business and industry, heavier taxation, and recognition of the demands of labor. The destruction of the Wilson coalition took place between 1917 and 1920. Labor became upset with Wilson's actions vis-à-vis the coal miners in 1919 and his inaction on the Plumb Plan to nationalize the railroads; radicals and antiwar agrarians were upset because of the war; isolationists in the party were disaffected by the Versailles treaty; and the important midwestern and western agrarian bloc became disaffected by the government's continuance of price ceilings on most agricultural products, with the exception of cotton, and the lack of attention to falling farm prices in 1920. In addition, the Hoover victory in 1928, particularly its impact in the South, made the Democrats give much more attention to party building. The Parker fight, coming as it did after the start of the Depression, was a ready-made issue by which the loyal opposition could distinguish itself from those currently in power and, at the same time, begin the healing process of reviving the Wilson coalition.[18]

After the introduction of the Dixon letter, much of the debate centered on the political nature of the appointment. Walsh (D-Massachusetts) commented that "the letter was apparently written immediately after the burial." Not only was the letter written immediately after the burial, but during the morning of March 13, Charles Jonas, Hoover's political operative, was already lining up endorsements for Parker. Overman was upset and demanded to know how McKellar got the letter. McKellar replied that it was in the subcommittee file. Borah gained the floor and read a telegram he and other Republicans opposing Parker had received. The telegram in part read: "We are building a great Republican party in the state. The lack of Judge Parker's confirmation will destroy our hope. Why let a fanatic like Green or the Negro element which we shall never tolerate prevail?"[19]

On May 5, two days before the vote, Blease entered several statements into the record from black people opposing the nomination, and Waterman (R-Colorado) defended Parker on the labor and race issues.[20] Then McKellar noted that his office had been broken into; he suspected Hoover's secret service agents. Smoot (R-Utah) and Brock (D-Tennessee) also noted that their offices had been broken into, but nothing of value in any of the offices seemed to be missing. Fess then attacked Ashurst (D-Arizona) on his statement to the press that "judgeships are being promised in return for a vote for Parker." Ashurst could not provide any evidence of this and had to retract his statement.[21]

Worried about the confirmation vote, Fess questioned the role of the NAACP in the Senate proceedings and struck out against its board of directors and some of its officers. According to Fess, "Du Bois was a Bolshevist; Pickens [director of branches], a Communist; Mary White Ovington, a socialist; John Holmes, a radical preacher; Oswald Garrison Villard, speaks for himself; Clarence Darrow, a defender of strikers in Cleveland's time; and Felix Frankfurter, a defender of revolutionary radicals." Not through with the NAACP, he also introduced a letter which attacked those mentioned above, and then Fess said that Florence Kelley had been "personally" trained by Engels and that Roger Baldwin was "Communist."[22] Fess and Simmons then moved to cut off debate and have the vote on May 7, at 12:30 p.m. Allen took the floor and inquired whether the senators or "outside minorities" were going to decide membership on the Court. He continued talking about Parker's confirmation as circuit court judge in 1925 and questioning why the racial question "which underrides the present controversy and is of deeper concern than any other issue in it, should not have been brought out?"[23]

Shortridge concluded the discussion with the statement: "If I thought for one moment Judge Parker . . . would join in any decision to deny to any colored man or woman his or her rights under the Constitution and the laws of the country, I would rather die here and now than to cast a vote for his confirmation."[24] In five years, significant changes in terms of the political standing of black people had occurred.

On May 7, Senator Hiram Johnson (R-California), speaking for the opposition, said:

> John J. Parker should be rejected as a judge of the Supreme Court, among other reasons, first because the background of the appointee is such that . . . it does not commend him as a judge of the Supreme Court. . . . Secondly, that the appointment is purely political in nature. . . . Thirdly, that the Red Jacket decision was a bad decision robbing individuals of basic rights much as the Dred Scott case had.[25]

Johnson had previewed his Senate comments to his sons in a letter, dated May 3. He wrote: "It is rather the irony of fate that if Parker is beaten, it will not be because [listing the reasons cited above] . . . but it will be because he said the Negroes were not fit for citizenship or to participate in politics."[26] Of course, Parker's supporters tried to counter all of these charges but to no avail.

The discussion of the role of blacks in the Senate debate did not end with the vote on May 7. Blease, who was close to being obsessed with the issue, related to the Senate the following story the next day:

> On the street car on the way to my hotel last evening there were two colored men sitting right behind me. One of them made the remark to the other, "Well, we gave the South hell

today." The other Negro asked how and the other replied,
"By beating Parker." A lady sitting beside me touched my
arm and said, "Did you hear that?" I said, "Yes, but I cannot
resent it because it is true."

He then inserted an editorial from the *Washington Post* dated
May 8, which read ". . . It was the Negro opposition that gave
the commanding position to the movement led by the progressives, aided in time in some degree by organized labor."[27]

Because the vote was so close, no single issue or argument
can be said to have been *the* issue that brought about the defeat
of the nomination. But when we look at the senators who
cast negative votes, we see that a new political configuration
had taken place, a configuration that included blacks (the
NAACP), southern Democrats, northern Democrats, labor, liberals, urbanized ethnic minorities, and progressive Republicans
(see Table 2).

While historians have tended to ignore the issue of race in
the defeat of Parker, a survey of newspaper coverage, both
black and white, Parker's own correspondence, President Hoover's assessment, NAACP national office and branch activity, and the political importance of the black vote in certain
states indicates that the NAACP campaign may have affected
from ten to thirteen votes.[28] Concurring with this view was
the *Atlanta Constitution*, which summed up the fight in its May
8 edition:

> Of the 49 votes cast against or paired against Judge Parker
> roughly 16 can be accounted for by the opposition to him
> expressed by leaders of Negro organizations. In at least ten
> northern and border states, however, Negroes cast a suffi-
> ciently considerable . . . vote to cause Senators to take account
> of them.[29]

The racial issue was of particular importance to senators from
Ohio, Maryland, Pennsylvania, New York, New Jersey, Massachusetts, Indiana, Tennessee, Illinois, Michigan, and Kentucky.
Thirteen of the twenty-two senators from these states voted
against Parker.[30]

The labor issue, by comparison, did not seem so strong as
it appeared in the earlier part of the debate. The *Atlanta Constitu-*

tion asserted: "The number who voted against Judge Parker because organized labor opposed him perhaps was slightly smaller than the number who voted against him because of the opposition of Negro leaders."[31] One reason for the diminution of the labor issue was the effectiveness of Parker's supporters in harking back, time and time again, to the idea that Parker was only following Supreme Court precedent. In addition, the Hoover administration provided documentation on the legality of Parker's rulings on labor matters, as well as Parker's own letter defending himself on the labor issue.[32] Increasingly as the Senate hearings continued, labor moved farther into the background compared to the race issue. A partial listing of senators prominent on the labor issue included Wagner, Borah, Norris, and McKellar.[33] The fact that all eight senators from Ohio, Pennsylvania, New Jersey, and West Virginia—areas of strong union activity—voted for Parker suggests the supremacy of racial over economic concerns. A number of these senators, however, were defeated in 1932 and 1934.

A third factor was the political issue. The Dixon letter and the blatant attempt to build a lily-white party in the South definitely had an effect on Senate Democrats. That southern Democrats would put themselves on the same side as the NAACP was interesting, but apparently politics was politics. Those southern senators who allowed party loyalty to outweigh regional loyalty included Barkley of Kentucky, Black and Heflin of Alabama, Brock and McKellar of Tennessee, Caraway and Robinson of Arkansas, Harris and George of Georgia, Sheppard of Texas, Trammell of Florida, and Tydings of Maryland.[34]

The fourth factor that contributed to Parker's defeat was the liberal vote. Some senators in both parties concluded that Parker's previous decisions on labor and his 1920 governor's speech bespoke a conservative whose judicial philosophy would only buttress that of the conservatives already on the Supreme Court. Because of the economic crisis the nation found itself in, new ideas were needed on the Court to counteract entrenched ideas. The Democratic part of this faction was led by Wagner and Copeland of New York, Walsh of Massachusetts, and seven other Democratic senators, all from the West (including the one Farmer Laborite vote from Minnesota). This issue was also of particular importance to the twenty-two Republicans

TABLE 2
Senate Votes by Party

For Confirmation
(Republicans)

Allen	Kansas	Keys	New Hampshire
Baird	New Jersey	McCulloch	Ohio
Bingham	Connecticut	Metcalf	Rhode Island
Dale	Vermont	Oddie	Nevada
Fess	Ohio	Patterson	Missouri
Gillette	Massachusetts	Reed	Pennsylvania
Goldsborough	Maryland	Shortridge	California
Gould	Maine	Smoot	Utah
Greene	Vermont	Sullivan	Wyoming
Hale	Maine	Thomas	Idaho
Hastings	Delaware	Townsend	Delaware
Hatfield	West Virginia	Walcott	Connecticut
Herbert	Rhode Island	Waterman	Colorado
Jones	Washington	Watson	Indiana
Kean	New Jersey		

Paired for Confirmation
(Republicans)

Goff	West Virginia
Norbeck	South Dakota
Moses	New Hampshire
Phipps	Colorado
Grundy	Pennsylvania

Against Confirmation
(Republicans)

Blaine	Wisconsin	La Follette	Wisconsin
Borah	Idaho	Norris	Nebraska
Capper	Kansas	Nye	North Dakota
Couzens	Michigan	Pine	Oklahoma
Cutting	New Mexico	Robinson	Indiana
Deneen	Illinois	Schall	Minnesota
Frazier	North Dakota	Steiwer	Oregon
Howell	Nebraska	Vandenberg	Michigan
Johnson	California		

Paired against Confirmation
(Republicans)

Brookhart	Iowa
Glenn	Illinois
McMaster	South Dakota
McNary	Oregon
Robison	Kentucky

For Confirmation
(Democrats)

Blease	South Carolina	Ransdell	Louisiana
Broussard	Louisiana	Simmons	North Carolina
Glass	Virginia	Steck	Iowa
Harrison	Mississippi	Stephens	Mississippi
Overman	North Carolina	Swanson	Virginia

Paired for Confirmation
(Democrats)

Fletcher	Florida
King	Utah
Smith	South Carolina

Against Confirmation
(Democrats)

Ashurst	Arizona	Kendrick	Wyoming
Barkley	Kentucky	McKellar	Tennessee
Black	Alabama	Pittman	Nevada
Bratton	New Mexico	Robinson	Arkansas
Brock	Tennessee	Sheppard	Texas
Caraway	Arkansas	Trammell	Florida
Connally	Texas	Tydings	Maryland
Copeland	New York	Wagner	New York
Dill	Washington	Walsh	Massachusetts
Harris	Georgia	Walsh	Montana
Hawes	Missouri	Wheeler	Montana
Hayden	Arizona		

Paired against Confirmation
(Democrats)

George	Georgia
Heflin	Alabama
Thomas	Oklahoma

Against Confirmation
(Farmer Laborite)

Shipstead	Minnesota

Source: Congressional Record, 71st Congress, 2d session, 1930, p. 8487; *New York Times,* May 8, 1930.

who voted against their party's nominee. Of these twenty-two, only five represented states east of the Mississippi.

The divided nature of the Republican vote on Parker was basically due to the division within the party itself. By 1910, eastern and midwestern industrialists had consolidated their control over the national segment of the party. Left out were the old Progressives who had come to power precisely to regulate this element, midwestern agrarians, and western progressives led by people such as Robert La Follette, William Borah, and Hiram Johnson. For these members of the Republican party, Parker's confirmation would only increase the power of the eastern bloc and, indeed, his decisions to date gave every indication of adding another vote to the conservative majority already on the Court.[35]

No one single issue proved decisive and indeed hardly any senator can be accused of voting against Parker on just one issue. In a larger sense, however, as one of Parker's supporters noted, the judge was only a "symbol," but a symbol around which a realignment of political forces was taking place in the United States. Those forces used the debate over the nomination to send a message to the president and the country that the policies of the old would have to be replaced by the policies of the new, if the United States were ever to get out of its current economic crisis.

The disparate coalition that had acted independently to defeat Parker was not particularly evident in the 1932 election. The Democratic landslide was so massive, the reaction against Hoover so strong, and Franklin Delano Roosevelt still so vague on his new vision of America that it is difficult to believe that people voted for something as much as they were voting against Hoover. By 1936, however, as V. O. Key wrote in *The Responsible Electorate:*

> The innovating period of the New Deal had pretty well run its course, and in that year the voters responded with a resounding ratification of the new thrust of government policy. Or, if one wishes to be cautious, the electorate resoundingly rejected the Republican alternative, which, as the campaign of 1936 developed, appeared to be a hysterical plea to return to the pre-1932 status quo lest the American system become a dictatorship.[36]

In the years between 1932 and 1936, Roosevelt's leadership and programs created a new coalition. In *The New Deal Coalition and the Election of 1948*, James Boyland observed that

> In 1936, Roosevelt reaped the full harvest of that division (rich versus poor). . . . It started with the old Democratic base—the urban machine and the south and border states. But then it reached out to constituencies beyond the old party. They included beneficiaries urban and rural . . . white and black ethnic groups . . . ideologically compatible progressive Republicans . . . ; union labor and blue-collar labor in general—almost the entire lower end, it seemed of the country's social-economic ladder.[37]

As Robert Wagner had noted in his Senate speech, Parker, who represented the forces of the old order, was incapable of viewing with sympathy the aspirations of those who were aiming for a better place in life. The anti-Parker coalition, although never articulated by a single leader in its ideological and partisan structure, was a precursor to the New Deal coalition.

Not only had the Parker fight transformed the NAACP into a leading civil rights organization, it brought about the recognition that the black vote in the North and in border states was a force to be reckoned with. This recognition strengthened the black insurgency movement that was still growing. The fight against the nomination of Judge Parker was a lesson in coalition politics that black and white people would learn from and draw upon for years to come.

4.

LONG MEMORIES

The Campaign against Pro-Parker Senators

Dramatic as it was, the battle in the Senate over Parker's confirmation lasted only six weeks. After twenty years in its struggle for existence, the NAACP realized that the Parker fight had brought it to a turning point. As a "nonpartisan" body, the organization had not previously supported or opposed candidates for office. The decision to do so required changes in its structure and the way it would carry on its work. The way in which the decision was made and accepted by the board was also an indication that, although the NAACP had "come of age," it would still have growing pains.

In the decision to continue the Parker fight by actively "opposing" senators up for reelection who had voted for Parker, the original role played by staffers at the national office had to change. As early as May 6, 1930, a day before the vote on Parker, Robert W. Bagnall, director of branches, had campaigned in Kansas against the reelection of Senator Allen. Bagnall probably took this option on his own; but he never received a rebuke from the board, and he continued to campaign against Allen for two months before the board made its "official decision" at the July meeting to work for the defeat of pro-Parker Senators.[1]

Meanwhile, without formally consulting the board on what was clearly a national policy issue, W. E. B. Du Bois, editor of *The Crisis*, listed all the senators who had voted for Parker. He gave their next election date and advised readers to "paste this [list] in your hat and keep it there until November, 1934."[2] Bagnall and Du Bois's actions indicated to the membership that the NAACP would continue to play an active role in forth-coming elections. Both of the national staffers were on safe ground in what they did because sentiment on the board was on the side of continuing the struggle. However, Walter White and the board realized that the organization's decision-making process now needed more centralization. White increasingly exerted his control over the national staff, causing contention with Chairman Ovington and Editor Du Bois. During his tenure as secretary, staff members never enjoyed the freedom of action given them under Secretary Johnson.[3]

White's confrontations with Du Bois are particularly illustra-tive of the situation White faced with the national staff after their successful defeat of the Parker nomination. Du Bois, who disliked White anyway, felt that as a "founder" of the organiza-tion he should have special status. Indeed, the early arrange-ments in the organization, which allowed him to operate out of a separate department, reporting to the board and not to the secretary, demonstrate the point. Additionally, Du Bois, through *The Crisis*, had attempted to push the NAACP from its legalistic approach for conquering race problems to one of economic uplift.[4] This unsuccessful campaign by Du Bois was tolerated by the board because of who he was and because *The Crisis* was self-sustaining, an important consideration for an organization constantly mired in financial troubles. Du Bois's actions in 1930 to push the organization to continue the Parker fight were also tolerated for the same reasons, as well as because the board was eager to continue what had been its most success-ful campaign to date. By 1933, however, White, with a now higher profile, demanded that the board exert more control over *The Crisis*, since it now needed monies from the general fund and it was the official magazine of the organization. As secretary of the Association, White sat on *The Crisis* board of directors and attempted to insure that it followed Association policy. This was too much for Du Bois, who angrily resigned in 1934, thus eliminating a clear and powerful opposition to White's authority.[5]

Another buttress to White's power and prestige was a mea-sure designed to oversee, or at least note, his activities. In

1930, Moorfield Storey, the founding president, died. His death and Johnson's departure created a vacuum at the core of the organization. The board formed a new Committee on Administration that would share executive power with the new secretary, and, they hoped, fill this gap.[6] However, because of White's prestige and recognition among the leaders of other organizations, because of the Parker fight, his influence with branch officials (many of whom later became board members), and his role in helping to select members of the board, by the mid-1930s, he was in control of almost all aspects of the NAACP (including the board, the national staff, and the branches). Even without the high visibility he received during the Parker fight, he might have been able to exert control over the organization, but he certainly could not have achieved it in so short a time. Not only had the struggle "matured" the NAACP, it had also "matured" Walter White.

At the July 14 meeting of the board, White reported that at the July 10 meeting of the Committee on Administration it had been recommended that "Pickens be sent to Kansas to take part in the campaign against Mr. Allen's reelection." Also at the July 14 meeting, the board decided to schedule the annual meeting of the Ohio State Conference of Branches for late July, so that "sentiment may be stimulated towards trying to defeat Senator McCulloch in the primaries. . . ."[7] The fight against the pro-Parker senators was officially started. The Association, however, was not going to place equal weight on the campaigns of all the pro-Parker senators. They were going to pick and choose whom they would most actively oppose. Allen (R-Kansas) and McCulloch (R-Ohio) would get the lion's share of attention from the national office. Two additional senators, Baird and Watson, were singled out for special attention. Other pro-Parker senators were to receive no more than publicity efforts and perhaps a speaker or two from the national office. The campaigns against the four senators listed above, however, were extensive campaigns coordinated by the national office but carried out largely by NAACP members in the states.

The senators selected to receive special attention were chosen for a number of reasons. They had Negro constituencies which the Association believed were sizeable enough to affect the election, if not also to bring about the senator's defeat. And not just coincidentally, these voters were potential NAACP members. All "selected" senators were politically vulnerable for various reasons. Finally, with the exception of Senator Allen, the selected senators came from states that had state conferences or would get them during the campaign in recognition of the states' large number of NAACP local chapters. As with the Parker fight, the campaign against pro-Parker senators would be used to garner memberships and funds to help sustain the organization while raising the political consciousness of black America and displaying a continuation of the political power demonstrated on May 7 in the United States Senate.

Not every black person, NAACP branch, or even national office staff member was pleased about continuing the Parker fight by opposing pro-Parker senators. On May 14, William Pickens, field organizer, sought to dampen the rising cries of voting against every pro-Parker senator. In an article entitled "Aftermath of Anti-Parker Fight," Pickens wrote: "Many of the Negro papers and leaders, elated over the defeat of Parker are saying something like this: Every Negro should vote forever against every Senator who voted for Parker and [presumably] for every Senator who voted against Parker." Pickens argued that blacks should be more discriminating in their voting, and he pointed out that Hiram Johnson (R-California) was also "anti-color" and that Shortridge (R-California), a pro-Parkerite, was "ten times safer for the Negro."[8]

Perhaps the most distinguished black individual to speak out publicly against the effort was Kelly Miller, a renowned professor at Howard University. Agreeing somewhat with Pickens's sentiments expressed in May, Miller wrote to White in November after the defeat of Allen and McCulloch, "I am as pleased as you are that Parker was defeated; but disagree widely with you in the view that the Negro should hound to defeat the otherwise friendly Senators. . . ." Professor Miller continued by saying that if a pro-Parker vote by a "lifelong friend of the race" means that he was an enemy then, "a negative vote by Senator Helflin . . . should make him our friend. . . ."[9] Miller then went on to explicitly express his support for Allen, Hastings, and Shortridge. He felt that black people were too weak politically to play the "vindictive game in politics," and that the Negro was not organized enough and the NAACP did not have enough resources to take on this job.

In October, the Boston branch sent a resolution to the national office, asking the national office to cease and desist from its political efforts. After acknowledging receipt, the board tabled the resolution to a later date. The decision had already been made to continue, and perhaps the board did not want to offend the Boston branch by a direct refusal of their request, or perhaps it hoped the Boston branch would forget about the request, in time. At the January 1931 board meeting, however, Mr. Joseph Loud, president of the Boston branch, brought up the branch resolution a second time, but again it was tabled. Not deterred, Loud brought the resolution up at the April 1931 meeting of the board. In White's report on that meeting, he noted that

> the whole subject of the Association's participation in the fight against Judge Parker and its opposition to senators who supported him was discussed at length, and the consensus of opinion was that the Association's participation in politics should be determined in each individual case as it arises. Mr. Loud withdrew his motion.[10]

The argument that some of the race's "friends" would be hurt by this kind of campaign, that the Association's resources could be better used elsewhere, and that these campaigns, unlike the Parker fight, would make the organization too political would be played out later at the state and individual level.

Nevertheless, the Association received a great deal of support from its branches, black newspapers, and individuals to continue the fight. The Baltimore branch, newly organized by Daisy Lampkin, among others, sent a resolution to the March 1931 board meeting which congratulated the organization on its leadership in the anti-Parker fight. The effect, said the Baltimore branch, was to "renew our confidence in the work now being done by our parent body [the fight against the senators]."[11]

The sentiment of some members of the Association had always been to continue the fight, as shown by the actions of Bagnall and Du Bois before the official policy decision. In a fund-raising letter to the branches dated May 8, Walter White wrote:

> We must realize, however, that the fight has just begun and we must not forget to thank those senators who voted against Parker nor must we forget those senators who voted for confirmation. Our slogan must be: Any Negro is a traitor to his race who votes for any senator who voted for Parker.[12]

Writing to branch officers on May 22, Bagnall, again pleading for funds and memberships wrote: "We need strong and large units in every community to arouse the Negro citizens and liberals to oppose those who opposed the cause of the Negro in this fight. . . . This is the best opportunity in years to secure membership."[13] As with the nomination fight, this campaign was to serve more than one purpose.

In an Association news release dated the following day, White went even further about the possibilities of what could be accomplished by the continuation of the fight. He said, "Let the memory of colored voters keep alive the vote of their Senators. . . . Let the colored vote register. . . . This is one of the sure ways to end lynching, peonage, race riots, and Jim Crow discrimination of all kinds."[14] After the Parker fight, the NAACP was becoming a much more political organization than before, although it remained "nonpartisan" on the surface.

Support for continuing the Association's political efforts also came from the Negro press. As early as April 26, the *Baltimore Afro-American* ran an article entitled "The Parker Case," which suggested that the fight against Parker be continued against his supporters.[15] After the nomination fight, the *Chicago Defender* and the *Pittsburgh Courier* ran articles congratulating anti-Parkerites and warning those who voted for him to beware of the negative consequences of their vote. The *Courier* article, entitled "Finishing the Job," also gave credit to the NAACP for carrying on the fight.[16]

The conduct of the campaigns varied from state to state. In 1930, only the Allen bid for reelection to the Senate from Kansas and the McCulloch reelection attempt in Ohio received serious attention.[17] The campaign against Senator Allen got started on May 6, when Director of Branches Robert Bagnall

conferred with the *Kansas City Call* about publicity efforts, and
on May 8 and 9, he lectured in Topeka. On May 10, he was
in Chanute, May 15 in Newton, May 17–18 in Wichita, and
May 19 in Winfield. The fight against Allen was carried on
in conjunction with NAACP membership drives in each of these
locations. From July 28 to August 4, Bagnall returned to Kansas
and addressed mass meetings across the state.[18] It was difficult sometimes to determine which took precedence—the fight
against Allen or the membership and fund-raising campaign.
But, both benefited from Bagnall's efforts, as revealed by a
Kansas City branch announcement on June 13: "We raised our
apportionment with greater ease this year than ever before
due largely to the publicity given the NAACP in the Parker
case."[19] In addition, the national office requested and received
extensive lists of black lawyers, ministers, and other prominent
individuals to be contacted in hope of soliciting support and
memberships.[20] Attention was also paid to the local branches;
a good example was a letter from Bagnall to Dr. F. O. Miller,
president of the Wichita, Kansas, branch. Bagnall scolded Miller
for not sending telegrams and letters to senators to oppose
Parker, and for not responding to Bagnall's attempt to set up
a speaking engagement with the branch. The members voted
Miller out of office.[21] The new branch president, John H. Grant,
produced what can only be called campaign literature against
Allen. The four-page handout, entitled "Take Your Choice: The
National Association for the Advancement of Colored People
or Henry J. Allen," said in part: "DO NOT BE MADE A FOOL
BY VOTING FOR ALLEN. And by disbelieving that this is
NOT between the NAACP and Senator Henry Allen."[22] It then
went on to recommend voting for Allen's opponent.

The importance of the role of Roy Wilkins, editor of the
Kansas City Call and secretary of the Kansas City branch of
the NAACP, must not be overlooked. Wilkins had corresponded
with Walter White early in the summer of 1930, convincing
him that Allen could be beaten in the Republican primary.
Wilkins was White's political eyes in Kansas, giving cogent
and valuable advice on Kansas politics and the best strategies
to be employed regarding particular candidates. Wilkins described Allen as a shrewd politician who had seen to it that
a black was appointed assistant United States attorney general,

with the announcement of the appointment and Allen's role
in it scheduled to be released just one month before the primary.
Also, Wilkins noted that many blacks knew and liked Allen
from his days as governor and through his newspaper, *The
Beacon*, where, according to Wilkins, "he always ran pictures
of colored people . . . wrote editorials about them, and gave
a 'break' on the front page with some news other than crime."
Wilkins was also aware of the stakes involved in this kind
of fight if Allen won. Attaching a postscript to his letter, Wilkins
wrote:

> The *Call*, of course, having been most outspoken against Allen
> would lose some prestige if Allen wins, but in their minds,
> the NAACP could lose the more. And too, the effect of the
> Negro vote would be further discounted. It would damage
> our people over all the country and mark the Parker fight
> for a "flare-up" rather than a genuine revolt.

Still, Wilkins argued that Allen had to be opposed because
he was Hoover's "key man" in the Senate nomination battle,
and his defeat in Kansas would not only be a rebuff to the
president but would be "the unmistakable signal . . . that Negroes resent the vote in the Parker fight."[23]

In an article published in the August *Crisis*, "The Negro Vote
and Allen," field secretary William Pickens reported on the
results:

> At the very most Allen received not one Negro vote out
> of four. This is very remarkable for two reasons: first, that
> the Allen campaign had gone the limit to enlist the Negro
> vote, by abundant money, by appointments of Negroes to
> prominent offices in Washington. . . . Second, that the Negro
> knew that the President, the National Republican Committee
> had been backing Allen.[24]

Allen won the Republican primary without Negro support
against three other opponents, but he lost in the general elections. The NAACP maintained its publicity campaign against
Allen throughout the general election. Allen's defeat resulted
from a combination of circumstances: he had been appointed
rather than elected; western Kansas farmers and labor unions
opposed him; and he was unable to consolidate a real base.

Although the NAACP claimed responsibility for the defeat, its role was only one factor. The defeat did, however, help build the image of the organization as a winner in politics. Writing in his autobiography more than a half century later Wilkins said, "As I look back on 1930, I can see that it was a turning point for me: more and more I wanted to shift from passively recording Jim Crow's knocks to fighting them." On August 15, 1931, Wilkins joined the national staff as assistant secretary in recognition of his press abilities and his skillful work in the Allen fight.[25]

A final note on this senatorial campaign. In 1931, at the annual meeting of the Kansas branches, the keynote speaker was Senator George McGill, Allen's successful opponent in the 1930 election. McGill, who took out a $10 membership in the NAACP, described Pickens's campaign in Kansas against Allen by saying, "When your distinguished guest campaigned here last year . . . he turned the colored vote to me which I could never have done myself."[26] This recognition of the Association's and Pickens's efforts must have only added to the heady feeling that, indeed, black people had become a political force to be reckoned with.

The campaign against Senator Roscoe McCulloch in Ohio was more extensive. The fight was directed by the Ohio Conference of Branches, a "revived" structure within the Association. By 1916, the NAACP's growth in membership and branches led many people on the state level to see the need for more coordination among branches. The first such effort was the establishment of the Great Lakes District Conference in 1916. Then in 1919 the Pennsylvania branches created a state conference. The creation of the Ohio Conference followed in the same year. However, the state conferences had lain moribund with little to do in the 1920s and had become almost non-existent. These state conferences were "re-organized" to make them effective weapons in the Parker fight. The Conference of Branches in Ohio was reorganized by Daisy E. Lampkin, Robert Bagnall, and Mr. C. E. Dickinson, president of the Columbus branch, who was to serve as the first president of the newly reorganized Conference. The date set for the organizational meeting, according to the July board minutes, was July 29 and 30, 1930. The invitation stated that the purpose of the organizing conference was "to organize at this time to defeat Senator McCulloch who voted against the Negro in voting for the confirmation of Judge Parker."[27]

Organizing to defeat McCulloch proved to be easier than similar efforts in other states. McCulloch, like Allen, had been appointed to fulfill an unexpired Senate seat and did not have a powerful base. In the 1930 election, Senator Simeon Fess, senior senator from Ohio, directed McCulloch's campaign, which received more aid from the national Republican party than any of the other Senate candidates.[28] The depressed economy and the related issues of farm relief and unemployment worked against McCulloch, as did his vote for Parker and his stance on Prohibition (McCulloch was a "dry" at a time when the state, particularly the urban areas, wanted to be "wet"). The national office of the AFL took a direct interest in the campaign, probably because William Green, president of the AFL, had been an Ohio state legislator and union leader and had kept very close ties to his home state. As early as May 21, 1930, James Wilson, general president, Pattern Maker's League, wrote to Thomas Donnelly, secretary-treasurer of the Ohio State Federation of Labor, saying that he had contacted Ohio Republican leaders seeking another candidate to replace McCulloch in the primary. He was informed that the Ohio GOP had already endorsed McCulloch and that sixty county parties had done the same. On May 23, Donnelly wrote to Green relaying the news and suggesting that since they were both Democrats, they should find a "recognized Republican labor leader to lead the fight in Ohio." On May 28, Green wrote back to Donnelly in a letter marked "personal":

> There has been great disaffection among Republicans in Northern Ohio over the appointment of Senator McCulloch. With that disaffection, along with the opposition of Labor and the Negroes of Ohio concentrated, it seems to me it will be impossible for Senator McCulloch to win [the primary].[29]

As happened in Kansas with Senator Allen, McCulloch's Republican opposition in the primary divided the vote so that McCulloch won the primary.

Meanwhile, the organization of the Ohio State Conference

of Branches was going forward under the direction of Robert Bagnall. Once completed, the conference could provide united action against cases of discrimination, increase the efficiency of existing branches, organize new branches, and take some of the work load from the national office (i.e., the campaign against McCulloch).[30] On July 14, Bagnall wrote a memorandum to the board informing them of his actions in Ohio and also informing them that the conferences in New Jersey and Indiana would serve as models for Ohio, with one notable exception.

> The Ohio State Conference [was] . . . to serve as an attempt to organize the state to seek to defeat . . . McCulloch in the primary. . . . While the Board has given its general permission for the trying of the experiment of State Conference . . . I am asking their specific approval of the effort of this Conference to organize for the defeat of Senator McCulloch. I need not state that Mrs. Lampkin and I will keep our hands on the machinery of the conference, so that it will not fall into the hands of professional politicians.[31]

In his invitations to the branches and prominent citizens to get them to attend the organizing conference in Ohio, the fight to defeat McCulloch was a strong drawing card.[32]

Bagnall wrote to Dickinson, conference president, a week before the conference meeting to discuss its political side. He told Dickinson to arrange rallies in cities all over the state with committees set to organize against McCulloch. And he issued a warning: "One thing we must be adamant about and that is that no funds shall be accepted from political parties or candidates to help in our political fight. We must keep our hands free so that we may be able to stand any sort of investigation."[33]

At the organizational conference, some of the delegates wanted to make it clear that they were opposing McCulloch not as an individual but because of his stand on Parker. Mr. B. F. Stewart from Columbus "pleaded for the courage to vote the Democratic ticket when the Republican party continues to betray the Negro."[34] Also, the state conference formally adopted a resolution opposing the election of Senator McCulloch. Mass meetings were held throughout the state, but McCulloch still won the primary, because he had a majority of the votes spread among several Republicans who sought the nomination.

Although it was clear to the national office, the state conference, and individual branches that the fight was going to continue on to the general election in November, Walter White wrote to Elliot Thurston of the *New York World* for advice on how to proceed. Thurston's advice and information had been very useful during the Parker fight in the Senate. White inquired whether or not the NAACP should work against McCulloch in the general election, and he indicated that a number of Ohio blacks opposed the continuation of the fight, because they "believe it will be a mistake to oppose McCulloch, who has been reasonably fair in his attitude toward Negroes up to the time of his vote for Parker."[35] Thurston replied that, if the Association did not continue the fight as promised, it would be weakened among blacks as well as in the nation in general. Thurston believed, however, that McCulloch would win the general election. White received a great deal of correspondence on both sides of this issue but continued the campaign against McCulloch.[36]

Despite the Association's opposition, McCulloch won the primary. Perhaps because Dickinson was nervous about how the new conference would work, or maybe because he recognized the growing reluctance within the state to continue the fight, he asked the national office to run the campaign. The board directed White to turn the offer down but to advise Dickinson that they would provide assistance in two forms—a loan of three hundred dollars, and speakers.[37] Walter White and Daisy Lampkin carried out the bulk of the national office's work in the state. White addressed meetings in Cleveland and Columbus.[38]

After McCulloch's victory in the primary, tactics changed. No longer was the NAACP just opposing McCulloch, but increasingly it was supporting Robert Bulkley, the Democratic opponent. White went to Cleveland to meet with Bulkley and made a long and detailed report of the trip lest there be any misunderstanding. In his report to the board, White let it be known that some black Republicans in Cleveland opposed the Association's activities. White wrote that he "made it clear to Bulkley that what the NAACP did in Ohio would not be pro-Bulkley but instead would be anti-McCulloch." According to White, Bulkley "seemed most appreciative of the indirect benefit to him which will come through the Association's efforts." For these "indirect efforts," Bulkley promised to support federal anti-lynching legislation, equal public school funds, and enforcement of the Fourteenth and Fifteenth Amendments.[39] On September 24, Bulkley attended a NAACP anti-McCulloch mass rally in Cleveland.[40]

On October 15, 1930, one month before the general election, a second conference of the Ohio branch was called.[41] This was an unusual move, but the Association had a high stake in this contest, and it smelled success. White chaired the conference, which was in fact an organizing committee for the election. The conference levied a special assessment of fifteen cents against each member, to be paid by their branches to finance the cost of the campaign—ten cents to the Ohio conference, five cents to the national office.[42] Mass rallies were scheduled throughout the state. On October 6, the national office sent out a memorandum detailing how the campaign should be conducted. It instructed each branch to keep a strict accounting of funds expended and to take the following six steps: first, have literature printed, giving the reason for opposing McCulloch; second, hold large public meetings to inform people of the opposition; third, canvas house-to-house; fourth, contact ministers and organization heads, so that they can put the case before their congregations and members; fifth, publicize activities through the local press; and sixth, send large delegations to White's speaking engagements throughout the state.[43]

During White's speaking tour of Ohio, "mysterious forces" added a new dimension to the campaign. When he arrived at the home where he was to stay during his engagement in Cleveland, he received a call from a female who invited him to her house to discuss a case in which the NAACP might have an interest. When he said he would meet her in the presence of witnesses where he was staying, the conversation ended. In Columbus, when he retrieved his coat after a speech, he found a whiskey bottle in the pocket. Fortunately for White, the Association, and the Ohio conference campaign against McCulloch, nothing came of these tricks.[44]

After the general election in which McCulloch was defeated, White received a very detailed account of the activities of the Ohio conference in the general election campaign. Altogether, the conference had produced 19,069 pieces of literature, and these were distributed to Ohio blacks.[45] The Negro vote in Ohio's large cities definitely shifted to the Democratic party, but several factors in the election influenced the shift. McCulloch was a Republican in the first general election after the Depression; he was a dry, opposing Bulkley, a wet; and organized labor opposed McCulloch's candidacy. But again, the NAACP was on the winning side.

The Association informed the Select Committee on Campaign Expenditures of its monetary contributions to all the 1930 senatorial campaigns: $896.11 in Ohio, $300.45 in Kansas, $13.45 in Delaware, and $3.20 in Rhode Island.[46] Efforts in the other 1930 races mainly involved publicity carried in *The Crisis* and local black newspapers. The Association did support some "old friends" in the 1930 election. Generally, this was done through publicity and/or a letter of support. Walter White sent a publicity article to the Democratic State Central Committee in Montana in support of the reelection of Senator Thomas Walsh.[47] The Association aided the Senate campaign of NAACP member Senator Arthur Capper (R-Kansas) through articles and letters.[48] Supporters of Senator George Norris wrote the Association asking if Pickens would campaign for him. Pickens could not go to Nebraska but assured Norris's supporters, "We are for Norris."[49] The NAACP also requested support from its membership for Senator J. M. Robison (D-Kentucky), who had voted against Parker, had helped sponsor an education bill with Capper that included black youth, and had praised the service of Negro soldiers in a speech on World War I veterans.[50]

Signs of the maturity of the NAACP and the depth of the concerns aroused on the Parker issue were the campaigns against ex-Senator David Baird of New Jersey in 1931, and against Senator James Watson of Indiana in 1932. The campaign against ex-Senator Baird was different from others in that Baird had retired from the Senate and in 1931 announced his candidacy for the governorship of New Jersey. Immediately, the NAACP moved to oppose his candidacy, and the campaign was carried out through the state conference structure. On March 6, 1931, the New Jersey State Conference passed a resolution opposing Baird's candidacy for governor and giving Baird's pro-Parker vote as the reason. Bagnall, as he would do in Indi-

ana, sent out a list of organizing strategies and campaign tech-
niques. There were, however, two major differences from the
campaign to be carried on later in Indiana. Because of New
Jersey's proximity to the national office, national officers were
more active in the rallies around the state. White and Bagnall
were much in evidence, as were Pickens, and Herbert Seligman.
But in the New Jersey campaign, about one-third of the nineteen
mass rallies were addressed by Roy Wilkins, more than by
any other national officer, a prelude to his later work. By this
time, the production of a campaign plan had become routinized.
Publicity materials and other campaign aids were based on
materials created for past campaigns.[51]

At the May 11, 1931, meeting of the NAACP's national board
of directors, White informed the board that Oscar de Priest
(the first black person elected to Congress since Reconstruction)
objected to the Association's opposition to Baird, saying that
he had been a friend of the race. However, a resolution was
entered and approved which read: "Voted, that the NAACP
stand its ground on the matter of opposing senators who voted
for confirmation of Judge John J. Parker."[52] In August, the national office produced a handout, *Why the NAACP Is Opposing
Baird in New Jersey*, which read in part:

> Nothing he can say or promise now can erase the *intention*
> of his vote then. He *intended* to vote for a man who believed
> Negroes should not have the right to vote. . . . Politicians
> believe colored voters have short memories and will forget
> easily. The voters of New Jersey have the chance to prove
> that they have long memories.[53]

The Bayonne branch also produced campaign materials. One
item, a pamphlet entitled "The NAACP Appeals to You," was
privately paid for, and it used the Association's name without
authorization. It gave reasons to oppose Baird but on the back
cover listed candidates who should be supported in the Bayonne
City Commission election.[54]

Dr. Vernon Bunche, president of the New Jersey State Conference, challenged Baird to debate White, knowing there was
little likelihood of this, but the challenge did garner some publicity for the campaign. White cautioned the officers to keep
strict accounting of their campaign expenditures, as these would

be reported to Senator Nye's committee on campaign expenditures, and any financial irregularities would damage the anti-Baird campaign as well as the NAACP.[55]

The New Jersey Republican party took this challenge a bit more seriously than had some other state Republican parties. In a letter to White, a local NAACP member quoted from a campaign pamphlet being circulated by the Republican party, which listed fifteen reasons why blacks should support Baird. Number fourteen pertained to Parker and was entitled "The Parker Vote Affair." Referring to the vote, it read, in part: "Little real analysis has been made of this situation. Organizations have used this Parker vote affair to raise money and gain prestige, but what actual good has the newspaper fight over it done the masses of Negroes? Little, if any." The real analysis, according to the New Jersey Republican party, "reveals that the entire fight was carried on through clever newspaper publicity." Then, getting a bit nasty, point fourteen concluded: "certain fancy-named organizations ask that we recall Mr. Baird's vote. Can these organizations take care of our employment relief through this winter or give our children State jobs? No they cannot."[56] The irony was apparently lost on the Republican party, which was going down to electoral defeat all over the nation because it could not provide relief and/or jobs.

In a memorandum to Seligman immediately after the election (which Baird lost), White instructed him on how to handle the colored press concerning the New Jersey election. Seligman was to emphasize the following points: the New Jersey conference led the fight with assistance from the national office; over 100,000 copies of "Why the NAACP Should Defeat Baird" were distributed; and Baird ran well behind other Republicans on the ticket. This discrepancy, White wrote, "was in large measure due to Negroes culling Baird who did not choose to vote for his Democratic opponent," thus emphasizing the image of the discriminating black voter.[57]

The campaign against James Watson had really originated in 1923 when he and other Republicans deserted the anti-lynching bill. Through the national office and through the state conference, Indiana blacks had been politicized. In addition, in August of 1930, there was a double lynching in Marion, Indiana, which shocked the community. This heightened political consciousness was demonstrated in a letter from Mrs. F. K. Bailey (president, Indiana conference of NAACP branches) to Bagnall in September 1930. She wrote:

> The Board of Directors met in Indianapolis and it was decided to hold the Conference in October. . . . Our great reason for the change is the fact that the state elections are held in the first part of November, and it is the consensus of opinion that a decided effort must be made to get the Negro in Indiana to stand together with their vote, as that seems now the only recourse left to us. . . .[58]

In October 1930, while campaigning against McCulloch in Ohio, White took a sidetrip to French Lick Springs and addressed the Indiana State Conference. After decrying the double lynching in August, White went on to say:

> The only hope for the Negro lies in political independence and we propose to do all within our power to that end. No wiser course can be followed by the colored voters of Indiana where the infamous Klan has honeycombed political parties and especially the Republican party.[59]

This speech and many others that White made in the aftermath of the Parker fight were important for two principal reasons. First, they often emphasized the ballot, as in this case, to the exclusion of the legal remedy, and second, they helped lay the groundwork for the switch in party allegiance. Identifying the Republicans as the Klanners made voting Democratic just a little bit more acceptable.

By 1932, although the ardor of the local black citizens over the anti-Parker campaign was still high, Bagnall was a bit more cautious and was beginning to become concerned over what effect these campaigns might have on the organization. Writing to White in early September, Bagnall stated: "I do not know whether it is well or not to instruct the delegates as to their attitude on Watson. While it is possible and desirable to defeat Watson, if any destruction in the Branches is to be the price, I would advise against it." After dismissing his own idea, he described the strategy to be used: "We must get the branches to actively organize as they did in New Jersey . . . with block and precinct meetings and earnest efforts to bring the people to the realization why they should vote against Watson."[60] In this effort as in previous ones, many forces in the state would be against the Republican Senate candidate.

Except for his concerns about possible branch troubles, Bagnall relayed the standard organizing memorandum to Mrs. Bailey with the added note: "An effort of this sort will make both parties realize that they must give more serious consideration to the interests of colored people."[61] And indeed, both parties had awakened to the new possibilities. Mrs. Bailey was offered the "colored women's organizer" post with the Democratic party. She turned this salaried position down so that she could remain "nonpartisan." But clearly, the Democratic party, at least on the state level, was awakening to the growing black insurgency movement and was seeking ways to capitalize on it.[62]

The Indiana conference received widespread publicity on its stand against Watson, not only from the NAACP Press Service but also from other members of the black press, most notably the *Pittsburgh Courier.* In an article entitled "Pro-Parker Senator on 'Spot' at Confab of Indiana NAACP," the writer noted:

> [the Conference] refused to endorse the candidacy of Senator James E. Watson, and to make their stand logical they unanimously voted to condemn President Hoover's candidacy. . . .
> The action of the conference precipitated a near riot when a few delegates alleged to be payrollers, attempted to frustrate the conference. . . .[63]

The near riot, more aptly described as vigorous discussion, was instituted by Mr. Gray, president of the Indianapolis branch, and Mrs. Grace Evans, president of the Terre Haute branch; both were strong Watson supporters. Both Mrs. Bailey and Bagnall wanted Gray's and Evans's resignations, as they felt that this campaign was too serious an issue to have a divided house.[64]

In his speech to the conference, White pointed out other reasons besides the Parker fight for blacks to switch party allegiances, most notably the Depression, which was affecting them disproportionately in terms of hunger and unemployment.[65] In the national Democratic landslide, Watson was defeated. Mrs. Bailey wrote to White, estimating "fifty percent of two hundred thousand Negro voters of Indiana voted . . . against Watson."[66] Bagnall replied to Mrs. Bailey: "Whether coincidental or not, it is gratifying that all over the country nearly all of the supporters of Judge Parker went down to defeat. In most cases of such defeat, the Negro vote very largely was cast against the defeated man, although in many instances it was not the deciding factor"—a much more somber and analytic assessment by the director of branches than in the halcyon days immediately after the Parker Senate vote.[67]

Robert L. Bailey, special assistant to the Indiana attorney general, wrote White after the election, giving his assessment of the election results. He, like Bagnall, was more somber about the implications, saying, "In my opinion, the magnitude of the landslide was so great that the Negro will benefit little at the pie counter of the hungry Democrats. In my judgment, he will benefit less than years past and the trend of the Negro vote, four years hence, will be back to the Republican fold."[68] He was correct about the benefits but not about the switch back. In four years more, blacks would be even more heavily Democratic in Indiana. Bailey also reported to White some of the successful Democratic tactics to win the black vote. Around polling places, Democrats put up signs that read "Hoover Nominated Parker," "Hoover Segregated the Gold Star Mothers," and "Watson Voted for Parker." Bailey wrote, "Colored voters were frequently approached by Democratic workers, some of whom were women with such cards pinned on their coats, and were told 'I know you are not going to stand for this' or 'I know you are against this' or 'You fought this too,' pointing to the card on their coat."[69]

The insurgency message clearly was not lost on the state's Democratic party, and they made the most of it. A postscript to this campaign and its significance for heightening the political consciousness awakened in the Parker fight was a letter written by Mrs. Bailey to White in April 1936. She told White "[she] believe[d] through state conference we should oppose nominations of Representatives who voted against civil rights bill in last legislature."[70] White replied, "Do not see any objection . . . as long as it is made clear Association opposition is nonpartisan."[71] The resolution passed the conference, and questionnaires were sent out to all candidates for the state legislature to determine their stand on civil rights in Indiana—another fruit of the Parker fight.[72] Black people were actively inserting themselves into the political process.

In a very perceptive editorial, the *St. Paul News* summed up the campaigns conducted up until then:

> Most significant is the growing potency of the "black vote." Since the World War scattered so many Negro families from the rural South into northern cities, this vote is being felt. It is no secret that the political power of these voters helped defeat Judge Parker for confirmation by the Senate. . . . Since then northern Negroes have successfully opposed three senators who voted to seat Parker. Allen of Kansas and McCulloch of Ohio were retired. In the defeat of former Senator David Baird . . . it was estimated that out of 90,000 Negro votes cast fully 75,000 were against Baird.

The writer connected this vote with political action on other trends and noted that in 1930 there were twenty-five lynchings, in 1931 only fourteen.[73]

By 1934, there were no strong senatorial campaigns. There were some publicity efforts, but basically the fight was over. The October 1934 issue of *The Crisis* recalled the Parker fight and the senatorial campaigns, noting that Gillette of Massachusetts and Goff of West Virginia were deceased, and that McCulloch of Ohio and Allen of Kansas had been defeated; Fess of Ohio, as well as Patterson of Missouri, Hatfield of West Virginia, and Kean of New Jersey were candidates in November. All lost in the 1934 election as Roosevelt increased his majority in both houses.

In the December 1934 issue, *The Crisis* published a final article entitled "Finish of the Parker Fight." The article, in part, read:

> The results of the November election marked the end of the fight on the senators who voted in May, 1930, for the confirmation of Judge John J. Parker. . . . All the senators who voted for Parker and who could be reached by the colored voters have been defeated. Of course, the colored voters alone could not have accomplished this feat. . . . The Negro voters . . . are to be congratulated upon their long memories. . . . The Parker fight marked the most sensational and significant political movement by Negroes in the last generation.[74]

The campaigns against the pro-Parker senators, which originally targeted all twenty-nine (excluding pairings), were not
notable for the damage they dealt to Republican political fortunes. But they were notable in strengthening the structure
of the organization. Soon state conferences would be applied
to most of the large states and would prove to be effective.
The tactics and strategies learned would be applied to other
campaigns and issues. However, most importantly, black America through the NAACP had once again inserted itself in the
political mainstream. Once having asserted its independence
and having decided for its own reasons to take a stand, the
black insurgency movement would only increase in power and
prestige. Black people could and did enter the Democratic party
in 1936, not as supplicants, but as political players who were
to some extent practiced in grass-roots politics and lobbying
activities, and who were led by individuals who had come
of age in a series of political campaigns.

AN ASSESSMENT OF THE PARKER FIGHT

Several questions remain about the Parker fight: What was the judicial effect of having defeated Judge Parker's nomination to the Supreme Court? Was a "racist" judge kept from the highest court of the land as his critics claim? Or, was a "liberal, fair-minded" jurist unfairly and unjustly denied the Supreme Court bench by misguided demagogues from black, labor, and liberal circles? Walter White wrote in his autobiography eighteen years after the Parker fight, "In Judge Parker's behalf I should like to add this postscript: Since his rejection, his decisions on both Negro and labor cases which have come before him have been above reproach in their strict adherence not only to the law but to the spirit of the Constitution."[1]

In 1942, Dr. Frank P. Graham, former president of the University of North Carolina at Chapel Hill, a southern liberal then serving on the National War Labor Board, suggested Parker replace Justice James C. McReynolds on the Supreme Court. Graham wrote, "his decisions on public power, equal pay for Negro teachers, and his recent labor decisions constitute a distinguished liberal record."[2] Later, the American Bar Association condemned the Senate's failure to confirm Parker as "one of the most regrettable combinations of error and injustice that has ever developed as to a nomination to the great Court."[3] In 1963 Richard Watson echoed many legal scholars in this regard: "When one evaluates Parker's record as Circuit Court judge, especially in the twenty-five years after his failure to reach the Supreme Court, one might have wished that he had been confirmed."[4] The question arises over whether in winning the battle, the NAACP lost the war. An examination of Judge Parker's judicial philosophy, his major court rulings, and his decisions in civil rights cases after his defeat shows that he was not a "friend of the Negro." From 1930 on, Parker's decisions slowed the cause of racial advancement.

The "precedent" justification used by Parker to defend his record during the confirmation battle is the "Catch-22" in legal stonewalling. The lower courts hold with precedents, and the Supreme Court often insists that only Congress, not the courts, can change the law. An almost total conformity to Supreme Court precedent was, according to Parker, only right and proper for a judge sitting on a lower federal court. In his defense of the injuction and yellow-dog issues during his confirmation hearings, he insisted, "I followed the law laid down by the Supreme Court and will not elaborate upon it. This is the duty of the lower courts and any other course would result in chaos."[5] In a lament to his former philosophy professor at the University of North Carolina, Parker went even further when he wrote:

> There can be no question that my decision in the Red Jacket case was strictly in accordance with the law as laid down by the Supreme Court. Had I decided otherwise I should not only have been reversed but rebuked by the Supreme Court. . . . The Supreme Court and not the lower court is the one to make change in the law which it declares.[6]

William Burris, author of the only full-length study of Parker's legal decisions, noted that the twists and turns of Supreme Court policy were Parker's twists and turns also. For example, from 1920 to 1937, there was a conservative majority on the Supreme Court. From 1939 to 1947, the Court became more liberal, more concerned with individual rights than property rights. The Court's rulings from 1948 to 1958 were two-tiered. The Court was very conservative on matters affecting national security, but it was increasingly liberal on individual rights, particularly with regard to civil rights, and Parker reflected these trends, with a few notable exceptions.[7]

Without question, from the time of his appointment in 1925 until the nomination battle, Parker's most controversial decision was the *United Mine Workers of America v. Red Jacket Consolidated Coal and Coke Company* (see chapter 4). The decision was based on Supreme Court precedent. From 1925 to 1930, Parker wrote seven opinions in property rights cases in which he held to strict adherence with Supreme Court precedent, even when he disagreed with the precedent.[8] Two years into his federal judgeship, Parker became de facto senior judge of the Fourth Circuit because of a death on the Court and the lengthy illness of the senior judge.[9] Where Parker found no precedent, he preferred to wait until the Supreme Court decided the principle and then apply it to subsequent cases.

After his rebuff in the Senate, Parker maintained his adherence to the conservative Court through 1937. However, in some areas where the Court had not articulated policy, he became a bit bolder and decided constitutional issues based on his interpretation of the Constitution. Two examples of this were his decisions in *Campbell v. Alleghany* and *Bradford v. Fahey*. Both of these cases came before his court in 1935, and both concerned the constitutionality of new economic programs. The first case involved Section 77B of the Bankruptcy Act of 1934 which allowed reduction of debt as part of a corporation's reorganization and the payment of those debts with nonmonetary resources. The plaintiff argued that this provision allowed for seizure of property without due process. Parker, in upholding the constitutionality of Section 77B, reasoned that the extraordinary economic conditions justified the use of greater power by Congress, and that it had the authority to enact such a law.[10] The second case involved Section 75 of the Frazier-Lemke Act, another bankruptcy provision being challenged on much the same grounds as the first case. Again, Parker upheld the provision using the same reason as in *Campbell v. Alleghany*.[11] On "Black Monday," May 27, 1935, when the Supreme Court mounted its strongest attack on the New Deal, it ruled the Frazier-Lemke Act unconstitutional, which reversed Parker's decision.[12] Throughout the rest of the New Deal, Parker ruled only within Supreme Court precedent.

From 1938 to 1947, when a slightly more liberal Supreme Court set policy, he followed its precedents strictly, with one notable exception. The exception was the 1942 case of *Barnette v. West Virginia State Board of Education*, more popularly known

as the "Flag Salute Case."[13] The plaintiffs were Jehovah's Witnesses who believed that forcing their children to salute the
flag was against their religious freedom as well as against the
First and Fourteenth Amendments. In a previous case heard
by the Supreme Court in 1940, *Minersville v. Gobitis*, it had
ruled, eight-to-one, that compulsory flag saluting was constitutional. Judge Parker in *Barnette*, speaking for the Circuit Court,
sympathized with the Witnesses and, in an extraordinary move
for him, said that there was an increasing trend in judicial
decisions to respect individual rights. He then sided with the
plaintiffs! This was the *first time he had ever gone against the
Supreme Court*. Parker felt that justice was more important in
this case than Supreme Court policy. He wrote:

> Ordinarily we would feel constrained by an unreversed deci-
> sion of the Supreme Court . . . whether we agree with it
> or not. . . . The Developments with respect to the *Gobitis*
> case, however, are such that we do not feel that it is incumbent
> upon us to accept it as binding authority. Of the seven justices
> now members of the Supreme Court who participated in that
> decision, four have now given public expression to the view
> that it is unsound.[14]

Here was a fine example of Parker's legal mind. He was able
to recognize shifting attitudes about social concerns by members
of the federal court system and to synthesize them into his
own thinking. His only other decision to take exception to Supreme Court precedent had been the *Bradford* case. But these
two cases demonstrate that despite his adherence to "precedent," on certain issues he would make exceptions.

From 1948 to 1958, the important cases before Parker's court
(outside of civil rights) involved the Communist party. In
Frankfeld v. United States and *Scales v. United States*, he followed
the more conservative Supreme Court in upholding the Smith
Act and greatly expanding governmental powers to prevent
"clear and probable" danger posed by Communists.[15]

Before 1930, Parker had no civil rights cases in his court.
But, from 1930 to 1958, Judge Parker concurred in or wrote
the opinion in six major civil rights cases. In all of these he
upheld the Supreme court precedent enunciated by *Plessy v.
Ferguson*, even after the Court had declared the Plessy decision

null and void! His first case involving civil rights was the *City of Richmond v. Deans* (see chapter 1). Parker, writing for the Fourth Circuit and citing a number of Supreme Court cases, ruled residential segregation law unconstitutional. His decision was later sustained by the Supreme Court.

The next case before the Fourth Circuit was *Alston v. Norfolk* in 1940.[16] In this case, Melvin Alston, a black school teacher, was suing the Norfolk School board for unequal wages. The NAACP, through Thurgood Marshall, William Hastie, Oliver W. Hill, and Leon Ransom, represented the plaintiff. The case was scheduled for June 1940, but the NAACP lawyers wanted it heard in special session because they were afraid the school would retaliate against Alston and other teachers before contracts were sent out in the fall. The Court asked to be advised if any retaliation occurred but maintained its original June date to hear the case. There was a suggestion that Walter White appear in the court with the NAACP attorneys, "but because of the Senate fight in 1930. . . ," he wrote in his autobiography, "it seemed to [us] that my appearance in the court would have been distinctly bad taste. . . ."[17]

On the basis of the Fourteenth Amendment due process and equal protection clauses, the NAACP lawyers argued that setting teachers' salaries by the school board was a state action and, as such, discriminatory salaries were prohibited. The Court agreed. The second question was whether or not the plaintiff's rights were infringed by the discriminatory practice; the court ruled "they [the black school teachers] . . . have the civil right : . . to pursue their profession without being subjected to discriminatory legislation on account of race or color." On a third point, the Court ruled that teachers could not seek relief from discrimination, even if they had already signed a discriminatory contract. The lawyers for the school board had argued the opposite. Parker, writing for the Court, agreed with the NAACP. Separate but equal was, at least, maintained through the Fourteenth Amendment and Supreme Court precedent.[18]

The next year, another civil rights case came before Parker, *Brotherhood of Locomotive Firemen and Enginemen et al. v. Tunstall*.[19] Representing Thomas Tunstall for the Association of Colored Railwaymen and Locomotive Firemen and the International Association of Railway Employees were Charles Houston, Joseph C. Waddy, and Oliver Hill. The Brotherhood had entered into an agreement with the Norfolk Southern Railway which denied black seniority rights and even the right to work at all. Charles Houston felt that, although the Railroad Labor Act did not relate directly to the issue of discrimination, the act constitutionally implied such protection. Tunstall's attorneys argued four main points: 1) that Tunstall and other black railwaymen should be represented by the Brotherhood who represented other railway workers; 2) that the union had to represent the interest of all the people in the union; 3) that workers experiencing discrimination had the right to seek redress; and 4) that unfair and illegal bargaining agreements should not be enforced. Parker, writing for the Court, denied all four points. The black railway workers could not recover seniority rights or loss of wages. The Brotherhood, according to Parker, had acted properly under the Railroad Labor Act.[20] However in 1944, agreeing with Houston's oral arguments, the Supreme Court reversed Parker's decision.[21]

Parker ruled in another civil rights case in 1947, *Rice v. Elmore*.[22] This case involved the constitutionality of the "white primary," a technique developed when the "grandfather clause" was ruled unconstitutional. In this situation, eligibility to vote in the Democratic primary (tantamount to election in most southern states) was a party function and not a state function. This case was on appeal from Judge Julius Waties Waring's Circuit Court in Columbia, South Carolina, where Waring had ruled that the white primary was unconstitutional because it violated the Fourteenth Amendment. George Elmore was the black defendant and Clay Rice the representative of the Democratic party. Elmore was represented by Thurgood Marshall, Harold Boulware, and Edward R. Dudley. Again, writing for the Court, Parker concluded, "The use of the Democratic primary in connection with the general election . . . and the denial to the Negro of the right to participate in the primary denies him all effective voice in the government. . . ."[23]

In 1949, Parker's court heard *Baskin et al. v. Brown*, another "white primary" case from South Carolina.[24] David Brown was the black respondent and W.P. Baskin a Democratic party official. This case was also on appeal from Judge Waring's court, as it involved the South Carolina Democratic party. Brown was represented by Thurgood Marshall, Harold Boulware, Robert Carter, and Constance Baker Motley. In this white primary case, the state, through the Democratic party, had given the responsibilty of running the primaries to private clubs, which of course blacks could not join. The appellants wanted a reversal of Waring's decision, because they thought he was biased toward them. Using the language in *Rice v. Elmore* and other relevant cases, Parker ruled the club-run primaries to be unconstitutional. Furthermore, the Court said that the evidence presented by the appellants did not prove the bias of Judge Waring against the defendants but, at most, "zeal for upholding the rights of Negroes under the Constitution and indignation that attempts should be made to deny them their rights."[25]

Up until this time, 1949, while one could have differed with some of Parker's decisions, perhaps wanting him to be more activist, he followed Supreme Court precedent, particularly with regard to *Plessy* and the Fourteenth Amendment. Parker was not the stereotypical southern, racist judge and, indeed, found in the Association's favor on some important cases, hence the favorable comments by Walter White and the American Bar Association's *Journal*. However, even though it would be difficult to find southern judges at this time to the left of Parker, with the notable exception of Julius Waties Waring, it does not mean that Parker was not impeding the cause of racial advancement by maintaining the status quo. By upholding *Plessy*, even as he was warned by other judges that *Plessy* was falling, Parker was signalling his intent to postpone or delay racial progress. Just how far he would go to maintain the status quo became apparent in the most important civil rights case to come before the Parker court, *Briggs v. Elliot* (1951).[26]

The *Briggs* case concerned Harry Briggs, a black parent who brought suit with other black parents against R. W. Elliot, school board chairmen of Clarendon County, South Carolina, and other members of the board. Representing Briggs and the other parents were the NAACP lawyers, Thurgood Marshall, Robert L. Carter, Harold Boulware, Spottswood W. Robinson, Arthur Shore, and A. T. Walden. Attorney General of South Carolina T. C. Callison, Robert McFigg, and S. A. Rogers represented the defendants. The case was heard before a three-judge panel:

Parker as Circuit judge; J. Waties Waring, District judge; and George Timmerman, District judge.

The plaintiffs' basic charge was that unequal and inferior schools were provided for black children, which was unconstitutional under the equal protection clause of the Fourteenth Amendment. Marshall argued along two lines. First, he demonstrated the unequalness for black children by the number and kinds of courses offered, the physical conditions of the school buildings, and the teacher-pupil ratio. Second, he argued that segregation was unconstitutional and detrimental to black children as well as to society as a whole. To prove this contention, the NAACP lawyers called numerous witnesses, including educators and sociologists. One of the more important witnesses was Kenneth Clark, whose famous "doll" studies demonstrated the effects of lowered self-esteem and negative self-images promoted by segregation.[27]

The defense, led by the South Carolina attorney general, did not attempt to refute the charges of unequal facilities, the differences were so drastic. McFigg said that a shortage of funds rather than racial discrimination was the cause of this situation. The state assembly was working to pass a bond issue to rectify the situation; hence, there was no need to desegregate to provide equal treatment for the black children. On the second point concerning desegregation, the defendants fell back on the Supreme Court precedent of Plessy.[28]

After hearing the arguments, the judges met in judicial conference. All three agreed that the action by the state assembly to increase funds for black schools satisfied the first issue of unequalness. On the second issue, segregation, Parker writing for himself and Timmerman, said, "It is equally well settled that there is no denial of the equal protection of the laws in segregating children in the schools for purposes of education, if the children of the different races are given equal facilities and opportunities. The leading case on the subject in the Supreme Court is Plessy v. Ferguson."[29] Judge Waring vehemently disagreed with this opinion. In his dissent, Waring acknowledged that a lower federal court could not overrule the Supreme Court, but he wrote that it was not necessary to overrule Plessy, rather just acknowledge that because of changing societal conditions it no longer applied. Because of the patently unequal school conditions, black children should be immediately admitted to the white schools, and *Plessy* would not have to be overruled.

In his dissent, Waring reviewed the history of the case, the history of the Fourteenth Amendment, the fight for black male suffrage, and the history of *Plessy*. He concluded:

> *Segregation is per se inequality.* As heretofore shown, the courts of this land have declared unequivocally that segregation is not equality. But these decisions have pruned away only the noxious fruits. Here in this case, we are asked to strike at its very root. . . . To me the situation is clear and important, particularly at this time when our national leaders are called upon to show to the world that our democracy means what it says.[30]

Because of the prominence of these cases, lawyers and judges wrote to Parker requesting copies of his opinions. One of those who wrote was Judge Walter Huxman, who said, "I know it will be helpful to us when we come to the consideration of the question in this case."[31] The case in this instance was *Brown v. Board of Education of Topeka, Kansas.*

Parker's reasoning, which relied so heavily upon *Plessy*, ran counter to his reasoning in *Barnette* and even in *Bradford*. In these latter two cases he acknowledged that changing societal conditions called for changing judicial attitudes even if it meant, as it did in *Barnette*, the overruling of Supreme Court doctrines. As Waring had pointed out in his case citations, particularly the Supreme Court cases of *Sweatt v. Painter* and *McLaurin v. Oklahoma State Rights*, *Plessy* was becoming more and more indefensible, not only on the grounds of "equal facilities" but also on the very grounds stated in Parker's court—those of self-esteem, self-image, and general well-being.[32] Parker was a learned, active jurist, as the cases in his court previous to *Briggs* have pointed up, but in this instance he appeared obtuse.

The *Briggs* case was immediately appealed to the Supreme Court. Since the NAACP was attacking school segregation in a number of courts, there were several cases around the country bearing on the same constitutional issues. The Supreme Court decided to wait until all the cases had gone through the appellate process before taking any of them. The other cases were

Brown v. Board of Education, Topeka, Kansas; Belton v. Gebhart, Delaware and *Bulah v. Gebhart, Delaware; Bolling v. Sharpe, D.C.;* and *Davis v. County School Board of Prince Edward County Virginia;* they were all combined under the *Brown* nomenclature.[33] School segregation was at the core of these cases, although the two cases from Delaware were a bit different. In those cases, the federal court had ordered the white schools to desegregate and admit black children.

The hearings began on December 9, 1952. All the plaintiffs were represented by members of the NAACP Legal Defense Fund. The main line of argument was that segregation meant not only inadequate facilities but in addition an unequal educational process, unequal motivation and educational atmosphere, and a sense of low self-esteem and inferiority on the part of black children. Because of the importance of the hearing, the attorney general of the United States, Herbert Brownell, was invited to participate. In an amicus curiae brief, the attorney general supported the plaintiffs but cautioned that in ruling in favor of *Brown,* desegregation would not and could not be accomplished immediately. The defendants stood on *Plessy.*

The Court met in judicial conference where everyone was free to speak his mind. There were strong differences on the Court. Justice Frankfurter was assigned the task of assimilating these differences and coming up with a set of questions to be posed to the litigants, so that some clarity might be reached.[34] Five questions central to the Fourteenth Amendment emerged from the conference: What rights and privileges did the Amendment guarantee? What were the intentions of Congress in framing the Amendment? Could the Supreme Court outlaw segregation in public schools? How should that be done? What would be the steps of implementation for such a decision? Responses to these questions were due in the fall of 1953. Unfortunately, Chief Justice Fred Vinson died and a new chief justice had to be selected. (Parker's supporters again urged his candidacy but with no success.)

The new chief justice, Earl Warren, a former governor of California (a non-judge rather than a member of the judicial fraternity), scheduled the hearings on the questions for December 7, 1953. After the arguments, the judges returned to their judicial conference, where it was clear that they were going to rule in favor of *Brown*. What was unclear, however, was just how the decision should be implemented. Warren and others were also concerned that the decision be unanimous. Any dissent from the majority would likely encourage massive resistance. The decision was announced on May 17, 1954. Writing for the unanimous Court, Warren said, "To separate them from others of similar age and qualifications solely because of their race generates a feeling of inferiority as to their status in the community that may affect their hearts and minds in a way unlikely ever to be undone." The Court's opinion also included the social scientific studies that had demonstrated the effects of segregation on black children. In conclusion, Warren wrote, "Separate facilities are 'inherently unequal.'" He then scheduled future hearings with the government, the NAACP, and the school boards for devising plans to implement the decision.[35]

On May 31, 1955, in what has come to be known as *Brown II*, Warren delivered another unanimous opinion from the Court concerning the implementation of *Brown*. Warren stated that the defendants should "make a prompt and reasonable start toward full compliance with our May 17, 1954 ruling." He determined that all the other cases before the Court which upheld segregation were to be returned to their respective federal courts for new hearings.[36]

Judge Parker issued his opinion in *Briggs III* on July 15, 1955. (*Briggs II* simply made the original decision comply with the *Brown* decision.) The opinion which became popularly known as the "Parker Principle" pointed out what he believed the *Brown* decision required and what it did not. Parker wrote,

> A state may not deny to any person on account of race the right to attend any school that it maintains. . . . But if the schools which it maintains are open to children of all races, no violation of the Constitution is involved even though the children of different races voluntarily attend schools, as they attend different churches. Nothing in the Constitution or in the [*Brown*] decision of the Supreme Court takes away from the people the freedom to choose the schools they attend. The Constitution, in other words, does not require integration. It merely forbids discrimination. It does not forbid such

> discrimination as occurs as the result of voluntary action.
> It merely forbids the use of governmental power to enforce
> segregation.[37]

Parker thus frustrated the meaning and force of the *Brown* decision. Richard Kluger, in *Simple Justice,* wrote of Parker "[he] set the standard for evasiveness by school districts throughout the South."[38] The NAACP was concerned that the Supreme Court might uphold Parker, but it still could not appeal because it lacked the necessary funds. Ten years after the Parker Principle was enunciated, the Clarendon School, the school in South Carolina that figured in the *Briggs* case, was still completely segregated.[39]

In 1956, Parker ruled as constitutional the North Carolina Pupil Placement Law which provided that students be placed in particular schools by school boards.[40] This law was just a pretext to resist the *Brown* decision. Parker, in upholding the law, believed that federal judges should not become involved in the operation of the schools or the enrollment of the students, and that black parents could not sue local school boards in states with pupil placement laws until they had exhausted all administrative remedies. Between 1954 and 1957, Parker wrote seventeen decisions concerning the implementation of *Brown.* In each of these, he found in support of his *Briggs III* decision, which encouraged massive resistance throughout the South.[41]

Judge Simon E. Sobeloff, a member of the Fourth Circuit, was disturbed enough about this practice to write Parker, hoping he might rewrite the Circuit Court's opinion in a particular case:

> I know how earnestly you have endeavored to moderate emotions in this area of race relations, and you have taken occasion to say in our court's opinions that which would help to lessen resistance to the Supreme Court's decisions. It was both true and useful to point out, as you have done in the past, that the law does not require wholesale reshuffling of pupils to compel mixing; but I am wondering if it serves the desired purpose to keep repeating this assertion. I fear that such repetition is less likely to allay fears than to encourage inaction.[42]

Judge Parker was not persuaded, and in the *School Board of*

City of Newport News v. Atkins (the case Sobeloff was referring to) the Parker Principle stood.[43] The other justice on the court who supported Parker in this decision was Clement Haynesworth.

At a crucial moment in American judicial history, and indeed, in the history of the United States, Parker chose not to fully support the highest court of the land after having done so in only a few notable exceptions all of his judicial life. By falling back on *Plessy* in the *Briggs* decision of 1951, Parker maintained his adherence to Supreme Court policy. Even though technically correct, as a learned, respected and active international legal scholar, Parker should have had no doubt that *Plessy* was wearing thin, as Judge Waring forcefully reminded him. The use of social scientific material in a court of law left Parker feeling skeptical, even though he had allowed it in his court in *Briggs I*. In this decision he expressed his view by writing, "Members of the judiciary have no more right to read their ideas of sociology into the Constitution than their ideas of economics."[44] Through his "Principle" he was trying to soften the blow that *Brown* dealt the South. After *Brown* and *Brown II*, however, finding justifications for his actions became very difficult.

Another factor which may have played a part in the Parker Principle was his political ambition, or more properly, his lack of political ambition after 1953. As mentioned previously, one of the reasons Parker became a Republican in the first place was because there appeared to be no advancement possibilities in the Democratic party of North Carolina when he offered his services in 1908, even though both his mother and father were Democrats. He then joined the Republican party and was assigned a party position where he worked on his first campaign. In 1910, he ran unsuccessfully for Congress; in 1916, he sought the office of attorney general in North Carolina; in 1920, he made his famous run for the governorship; and in 1924, he was National Republican Committeeman from North Carolina.[45]

Although not openly political after his appointment to the federal bench in 1925, he was a political operative. When a federal judgeship became available in 1922 in eastern North Carolina (Parker, from the town of Charlotte, was not eligible), he wrote to President Harding requesting that the judgeship

not go to a Democrat, because Democrats had already selected
more than their fair share of judges. Parker wrote, "I think
that the fair administration of justice is best preserved by the
appointment of Republican lawyers to the Federal bench."[46]
In 1925, he disdained the thought of a district judgeship, saying
"I am temperamentally unfit for a judgeship. I feel quite certain
that I would not be a good trial judge."[47] When a vacancy
occurred on the Fourth Circuit, he was, however, very interested, although he did not want "to appear in any sense as
a candidate for the position."[48] Since the Fourth Circuit included
Virginia, Maryland, West Virginia, North Carolina, and South
Carolina, he feared a great deal of competition. Parker pointed
out to Republican connections in Washington that Virginia and
Maryland were already represented on the court; West Virginia
as well as Virginia and Maryland were common law states;
and North and South Carolina were code law states. Hence,
a judge from either of the Carolinas would add diversity, and
since the last judge was from South Carolina, the appointment
should be made from North Carolina.[49] In North Carolina, his
only competition was an older Republican judge about whom
Parker wrote: "I do not think there is any possibility of Judge
Bynum being appointed, and I feel that the only chance of
my being appointed is to have the unanimous support of the
bench and bar of these states."[50] He received that support and
wrote to both of his senators, Lee Overman and Furnifold
Simmons, thanking them for their support.[51]

He played his political games again during his confirmation
hearings for the Supreme Court. While the nomination was
still before the judiciary subcommittee and had already drawn
fire from the NAACP, he wrote David Blair, a Republican political operative from North Carolina, a defense of his 1920 governor's speech to be passed along to friendly senators.[52] Then
Parker agreed, through his supporters, to testify before the
judiciary committee on April 21, an unprecedented move by
a Supreme Court nominee at that time.[53] Throughout the hearings, Parker was in constant contact with his supporters, dis-
cussing strategy and possibilities.[54] Toward the end of the fight,
Charles Taylor of the Friends Society met with Parker to draft
a letter which would disavow his 1920 speech. Parker wrote
the letter, but neither Walter White nor Taylor was convinced

of its sincerity or that it had gone far enough.[55] Noting all of this activity by Parker on his own behalf, the *New York Times* wrote that he was "too much like a candidate for the office of sheriff."[56] Indeed, it is hard to believe that Parker was campaigning so openly for a position he had once termed "the highest position to which human beings can aspire."[57]

For Parker the rejection of his nomination had something of a silver lining. Writing to a professor and old friend at Chapel Hill, Parker said, "My appointment by the President, even though not confirmed, will probably give me an outstanding position as a circuit judge and will cause my opinions to be more carefully scrutinized than they would otherwise be."[58] Parker believed that he would eventually become a Supreme Court Justice, as he told his brother in a letter in late May 1930: "I believe that eventually I shall be appointed to the Supreme Court and confirmed."[59] His name was put forward for nomination to almost every open seat on the Supreme Court from 1930 to 1953.[60] He was aware of these activities on his behalf by his supporters and did not dissuade them. In addition, Parker maintained an extensive correspondence with every president from Hoover to Eisenhower. The correspondence consisted of Parker's appreciation for their speeches and their policies and called attention to his major speeches and articles.[61] This did not hurt Parker when a vacancy on the bench occurred, but in the end it did not help.

When he did not receive the nomination in 1953 that eventually went to Earl Warren, he probably realized that he would never be on the Supreme Court. There was no need to temper himself on the race issue anymore, hence the *Briggs* dictum. Technically correct but certainly not in the spirit of *Brown*, it reflected his personal, political and judicial view of the race situation. Race mixing was not to be condoned or encouraged. In a letter, which Parker never sent, to Senator Henry J. Allen after the Senate fight in 1930, he wrote, "In the first place there can be no such thing as social equality or intercourse between the races. In the second place the participation by the Negro in politics is a source of evil and danger to both races and is not desired by wise men in either race."[62] By 1955, Parker had not changed. Only the possibility of appointment to the Court kept his true feelings and beliefs in check.

The NAACP had been correct in fighting his nomination. Although he was consistent with the Supreme Court (where policy had been established with the notable exception of *Barnette*), he could not fully support *Brown*. Throughout his judicial career in cases dealing with racial questions, Parker was unwilling to push for change. None of his opinions ever increased black civil rights; at best, they maintained the status quo. His constant referral to *Plessy*, even as he knew it was falling, gave a good indication of his views on race matters.

One wonders if Chief Justice Warren would have been able to get a recalcitrant Parker to agree to a unanimous decision. Given Parker's record after *Brown*, one thinks not. Indeed, Parker's feelings on race overwhelmed even the most important tenet of his judicial philosophy—adherence to Supreme Court doctrine. The NAACP had no way of knowing what his decisions would be twenty-five years after the confirmation fight, but Parker's background, his governor's campaign, his judicial philosophy, and his political ambitions indicate that in the Association's struggle for change Parker would have been more of a hindrance than a help. By opposing his nomination in 1930, the NAACP won a battle that ultimately enabled it to become a leading force for the political, economic, and social equality of all Americans.

The decision by the NAACP from its earliest inception to pursue a legal and educational approach to redressing black grievances had had fateful consequences. The adoption and initial successes of this approach committed the Association to a rigorous examination of the nation's most important legal institution—the United States Supreme Court and particularly those individuals nominated to the court. It is this scrutiny that led to the challenge of the Parker nomination and its subsequent defeat. The process of defeating Judge Parker helped black Americans make two other decisions: to switch to the Democratic party; and to continue to investigate nominees to the Supreme Court. Both strategies have had impressive results, but each has also had drawbacks.

Having supported the national Republican party (by a majority vote) in every presidential election from 1860 to 1932, black voters deserted to the Democratic presidential ticket in 1936, a switch that was predictable but nonetheless stunning. Black voters had been neglected, scorned, and insulted by the Republican party since the late 1870s. Except for a few northern cities, the Democratic party had made little or no attempt to bring black voters within its ranks. The prevailing assumption of white Republicans and Democrats was that lethargy, political bosses, allegiance to the memory of Lincoln, and the apathy and hostility of the Democratic party would keep black voters rooted in their traditional political roles.

When the switch did come, contemporary social scientists explained it in terms of the attraction of Franklin D. Roosevelt's New Deal welfare state, the influence of Eleanor Roosevelt, and an empathetic bonding between a handicapped president and a handicapped people. Current historians have used variants of these themes to explain the switch, citing economic assistance received from the New Deal and/or the recognition of race and rights as a substantive matter.[1] Both of these arguments are valid to a certain extent. However, an aspect that both arguments overlook is the question of what black people were doing for themselves, not just what was being done to them by the New Deal, the Republican party, and the Democratic party.

The majority of the black population still lived in the South at this time. With the exception of a few black Democrats in the 1890s, most black voters were Republican. The movement in the South for black disfranchisement meant that very few blacks were even eligible to vote, and the lily-white movement did not leave much for which to vote. With the start of the Great Migration from the South, blacks had more opportunity for eligibility to vote, and in their new environment, the traditional appeal of the Republican party had little relevance. The "new" Democratic party at least appeared more inviting. What was needed was some experience of participation in the political process. The Parker nomination fight and the fight against pro-Parker senators was a major step in helping to move the black electorate from the Republican column into the Democratic column.

The importance of the NAACP's campaign against pro-Parker senators was initially overblown. In most cases by 1934, the NAACP freely admitted that other factors than the black vote made the difference in the defeat of the senators. However, the value of these campaigns to the politicization process of black people was tremendous. For the NAACP the campaigns continued to provide leadership training, not only for the national office staff (including Roy Wilkins, who came to the national office during these campaigns) but also for local leaders who were able to adopt these strategies and tactics to local issues and concerns. In the campaigns against Parker's supporters in the Senate, the NAACP positioned itself as the political voice of black Americans. The Association defined the issue at stake. Blacks could see that politics was a matter of choice, not the "electoral slavery" into which the party of Lincoln had led them, and that after all it might be a bit more acceptable to vote for the party of Blease, Vardaman, and lynching.

Once having switched to the Democratic party, the black electorate has remained firmly entrenched within that party, proving to be a crucial element to Democratic victories in 1948, 1960, and 1976, and has used this support to claim a voice in Supreme Court nominations.[2] Following the defeat of the Parker nomination, the black electorate has tried to flex its collective muscle on other Supreme Court nominees and has been influential in three other cases: the nominations of Clement Haynesworth, G. Harold Carswell, and Robert Bork. It should be emphasized that the black electorate (as represented by their senators and the NAACP) although crucial could not have defeated these nominees alone. However, without opposition from the black community, the nominees might well have been seated on the Supreme Court.

All three battles bear remarkable similarity to the Parker fight with one difference. When Judge Parker was defeated, blacks were just emerging into the political mainstream. There were important Supreme Court decisions to be preserved. But by 1987, with the nomination of Judge Robert Bork, the black community, in retrenchment and retreat during the Reagan years, saw the possibility that advances made in the 1960s and 1970s were at stake. It was a mark of how desperate the black electoral community had become that, at the time of the bicentennial celebration of the Constitution of the United States, black people looked to the least democratic of our governmental bodies as a guarantor of their rights.

This dependence on the Court has grown out of two circumstances. First, the NAACP, through its legal strategy, has continued to win and consolidate civil rights through the Court. *Brown* was only the first of many decisions handed down by the Court in the modern civil rights era. By 1969, the Supreme Court had upheld the 1957 Civil Rights Act, the 1964 Civil Rights Act, and the 1965 Voting Rights Act, and it would soon uphold the 1968 Civil Rights Act. In addition, the Court had finally outlawed poll taxes, defeated anti-miscegenation laws, insured that indigent defendants were guaranteed counsel, and ruled that racially inspired gerrymandering was unconstitutional. It appeared, in 1969, that much of the civil rights agenda had been voted by Congress and confirmed by the Supreme Court.

However, beginning in 1966, the Supreme Court liberal coalition led by Chief Justice Earl Warren was beginning to suffer losses in civil rights which often put Warren and his liberal colleagues on the defensive. With Earl Warren's retirement in 1969 and his replacement by Warren Burger, a Nixon conservative, the Supreme Court was closely balanced between the liberal faction (Douglas, Black, Marshall, Brennan, Fortas) and the conservative faction (Burger, Harlan, Stewart, White), although Justice Black increasingly switched to the conservative side on civil rights issues. The appointment of Thurgood Marshall was not only an acknowledgment of his work for civil rights but also a realization that a black voice was needed on the Court, if it were to continue as a fair and impartial body. With the forced resignation of Justice Fortas in 1969, the "Jewish seat" was open and the balance on civil rights was clearly at risk.[3]

President Nixon, like President Hoover, also had had a "southern strategy." In gratitude for southern support, he kept his promise to appoint a "strict constructionist" to the Court. The person he chose to replace Abe Fortas was Clement F. Haynesworth, chief judge of the Fourth Circuit Court of Appeals, Richmond, Virginia—Parker's old court. Haynesworth, a Democrat, had been appointed by President Eisenhower in 1957 and had become a Republican in 1964.

At first, it appeared Haynesworth would be acceptable to a Democratic Senate: he was considered a moderate to conservative on civil rights as well as criminal rights. But again, like the Parker nomination, critics looked into Haynesworth's record and found grounds for objections. The NAACP and the Leadership Conference on Civil Rights found Haynesworth to be unsympathetic to black people, announced they would oppose the nomination, and launched another grass-roots lobbying campaign directed against the Senate. In addition, some senators saw the nomination as a political payoff to the South and a reward to Senator Strom Thurmond for his support of Richard Nixon over George Wallace in 1968.

The nomination was also opposed by labor. In seven cases, all overturned by the Supreme Court, Haynesworth had sided with management over labor. There was also a question of ethics. Haynesworth owned stock in a vending machine company that serviced mills owned by Deering Milliken, Inc. and had found in favor of Milliken against the Textile Workers Union in their attempt to prevent plant closings. Haynesworth had also purchased shares in the Brunswick Corporation during litigation in his court. Although many did not see these ethical violations as extremely serious, they did carry some weight because of the forced resignation of Fortas for ethical violations.

On November 21, 1969, the Senate defeated the Haynesworth nomination, forty-five to fifty-five, because of a combination of factors, including race, labor, political, and ethical issues. The NAACP claimed a major part of the credit.[4]

President Nixon reacted to the defeat by promising to appoint another southern "strict constructionist." He chose G. Harold Carswell, a member of the Fifth Circuit Court of Appeals in New Orleans. Carswell's nomination initially was met with little opposition. Few believed after the Haynesworth fight that the Senate was in the mood to challenge the President again. The only significant opposition raised to Carswell was by the NAACP. Its objection was based on a campaign speech made by Carswell in 1947. In the speech he said, "I am a Southerner by ancestry, birth, training, inclination, belief, and practice. I believe that segregation of the races is proper and the only practical and correct way of life in our states."[5] Carswell sought to dismiss these statements as political rhetoric which he now strongly opposed. After Carswell's record surfaced, lawyers who had practiced before him detailed his hostility to civil rights laws and blacks. Questions then began to emerge about his qualifications.

Although the Senate Judiciary Committee moved his nomination out of committee, thirteen to four, his opponents hoped he could be defeated if they could stall the Senate debate long enough to gather more damaging information. Fortunately for Carswell's opponents, the Senate did delay debate over the nomination as they wrestled with the 1970 Voting Rights Act, and more damaging information did emerge. In 1956 Carswell had helped convert a public golf course to a private course, allegedly to avoid desegregation. Carswell denied that this action was for discriminatory reasons, but few believed him. In 1966 he sold property with a restrictive covenant barring future sale to black people. These charges combined with growing concern over his legal competency led the Senate to defeat his nomination, forty-five to fifty-one.[6] President Nixon finally appointed William Rehnquist, a moderate conservative with no apparent major liabilities in his background.

The fourth time in this century that the black vote has been instrumental in denying a person a place on the Supreme Court was the 1987 Senate fight over the nomination of Judge Robert

H. Bork, again reminiscent of the Parker fight. Bork was well known as solicitor general in the Nixon administration and as a judge on the district court in Washington, D.C. In the Bork struggle, black opposition was based on the judge's views and on the belief that a Reagan nominee spelled only trouble for black America. The Reagan years were not good years for civil rights and black America. President Reagan had run on a platform of reduced spending on social programs and a lessened role for the federal government in every facet of American life. Besides support from right wing conservatives and traditional Republicans, Reagan was able to garner the support of white blue collar workers who supported his stand against affirmative action and equal opportunity programs.

In eight years in office, Reagan appointed only one black cabinet officer, Samuel R. Pierce, as head of Housing and Urban Development. In 1981 the president interfered politically with the United States Civil Rights Commission, replacing its chairman with Clarence Pendleton, a black Republican from California who opposed affirmative action and the government's equal opportunity programs. Reagan also attempted to remove three of the Commission's members but was stopped by countermoves in Congress. However, for both terms of his administration the Commission was almost totally ineffective in the areas of civil rights.

Equally alarming to black America was the president's attempt in 1982 to allow tax-exempt status for two schools, Bob Jones University and Goldsboro Christian School, which openly practiced racial discrimination. Public and congressional outcry stopped Reagan's action. Also in 1982, when Congress debated the renewal of the 1965 Voting Rights Act, President Reagan initially opposed its renewal but finally gave it token support. And although Reagan did sign the bill in 1983 making Martin Luther King, Jr.'s birthday a national holiday, again he appeared to do so reluctantly.

Given Reagan's records on appointments and his reluctance to support affirmative congressional actions, any Court nominee would receive a close scrutiny from black America and its institutional representatives. Reagan's first two Supreme Court appointments, Associate Justice William Rehnquist, appointed chief justice upon the retirement of Warren Burger, and Antonin Scalia, a conservative named to replace Rehnquist, received some opposition from civil rights groups and their supporters. But since these appointments basically maintained the status quo on the Court, it was impossible to defeat their nominations.

However, with Reagan's third Supreme Court appointment, to replace retiring Justice Lewis Powell, the stakes became higher. Powell was considered a moderate conservative who, while not advancing civil rights, had never advocated a roll back of the gains made and consolidated by the Warren and Burger courts. Judge Bork, who was proudly proclaimed by Reagan as a person who would tilt the balance and roll back the "activism" of the Warren court, was clearly unacceptable to black America and the NAACP.

As in the Parker fight, the nominee was objectionable to more than just black Americans. For the National Organization of Women, supporters of abortion rights, and other women's rights groups, Bork was unacceptable because he believed that *Roe v. Wade* was an "unconstitutional decision." Bork also criticized the Supreme Court's 1965 decision in *Griswold v. Connecticut*, saying that he could find no right to privacy or right to contraceptive use in the Constitution. Bork's support of the death penalty and a weakening of the evidential exclusionary rules raised great concern for legal rights advocates. Organized labor and conservation groups opposed Bork's nomination because of his rulings in district court which tended to weaken federal regulation of business in its conduct of labor negotiations and its effect on the environment.[7]

But the single greatest concern of Bork critics was his stand on civil rights. He opposed the 1964 Civil Rights Act, although he later changed his position. He had a "theoretical" objection to the *Brown* decision, and he opposed the 1963 public housing accommodations bill and affirmative action. Clearly, President Reagan was standing on firm ground when he chose Bork to "roll back" the advances of the Warren Court. For black voters, given the damage of the Reagan years and Bork's record, a vote for Bork was a vote against black people.

The White House strategy on Bork was based on the notion that women's rights and pro-choice groups, labor, and liberal critics could be defeated. As in the Parker fight, possible black and civil rights objections were dismissed. Had not Reagan been re-elected in 1984 on the same themes of opposing social programs and affirmative action? Black criticism had had little effect on his re-election campaign.

By early October what the president and his advisors had assumed would be a relatively easy confirmation was in serious trouble. The White House had based its tactics on a "southern strategy." That is, by holding onto their Republican base they hoped to secure enough votes from defecting southern Democrats to secure the confirmation. What the Republicans had not thought through were the implications of the 1986 congressional elections, in which a new breed of southern Democratic senators strongly supported by black votes had been elected, often replacing Republican senators who had come in on Reagan's coattails in 1980. In addition, Reagan had vigorously campaigned against these senators in a vain attempt to maintain his party's 1980 momentum in the South.

But one after another southern Democratic senators came out against Bork: Terry Sanford of North Carolina, David Pryor of Arkansas, J. Bennet Johnston of Louisiana, and Lloyd Bentsen of Texas. These senators all noted Bork's stand on civil rights as the main reason for their opposition. Senator Bentsen's comments were typical of the group when he said, "My concern is that you could turn back the clock on civil rights. We've already fought those fights and we're happy with the outcome."[8] Judge Bork's nomination was defeated forty-two to fifty-eight.[9] Again, as in the Parker fight, it had been a coalition of groups which had brought about the judge's defeat, but the black vote expressed through its elected representatives had been crucial.

Black voters saw Reagan's nomination of Bork as a further retreat from civil rights. They voiced their opposition from all parts of the nation, particularly from the South. Again, black people had won. The NAACP should be given major credit for its part in this fight. Despite continued criticism of the NAACP by some blacks activists and others, the nation's oldest civil rights organization has proved invaluable in the quest for black freedom and dignity.

"THE CALL"
A LINCOLN EMANCIPATION CONFERENCE

To Discuss Means for
Securing Political and Civil Equality
for the Negro

The celebration of the centennial of the birth of Abraham Lincoln widespread and grateful as it may be, will fail to justify itself if it takes no note and makes no recognition of the colored men and women to whom the great emancipator labored to assure freedom. Besides a day of rejoicing, Lincoln's birthday in 1909 should be one of taking stock of the nation's progress since 1865. How far has it lived up to the obligations imposed upon it by the Emancipation Proclamation? How far has it gone in assuring to each and every citizen, irrespective of color, the equality of opportunity and equality before the law, which underlie our American institutions and are guaranteed by the Constitution?

If Mr. Lincoln could revisit this country he would be disheartened by the nation's failure in this respect. He would learn that on January 1st, 1909, Georgia had rounded out a new oligarchy by disfranchising the negro after the manner of all the other Southern states. He would learn that the Supreme Court of the United States, designed to be a bulwark of American liberties, had failed to meet several opportunities to pass squarely upon this disfranchisement of millions by laws avowedly discriminatory and openly enforced in such manner that white men may vote and black men be without a vote in their government; he would discover, there, that taxation without representation is the lot of millions of wealth-producing American citizens, in whose hands rests the economic progress and welfare of an entire section of the country. He would learn that the Supreme Court, according to the official statement of one of its own judges in the Berea College case, has laid down the principle that if an individual State chooses it may "make it a crime for white and colored persons to frequent the same market place at the same time, or appear in an assemblage

From Charles Flint Kellogg, *NAACP: A History of the National Association for the Advancement of Colored People* (Baltimore: Johns Hopkins University Press, 1967), pp. 297–99.

of citizens convened to consider questions of a public or political nature in which all citizens, without regard to race, are equally interested." In many States Lincoln would find justice enforced, if at all, by judges elected by one element in a community to pass upon the liberties and lives of another. He would see the black men and women, for whose freedom a hundred thousand soldiers gave their lives, set apart in trains, in which they pay first-class fares for third-class service, in railway stations and in places of entertainment, while State after State declines to do its elementary duty in preparing the negro through education for the best exercise of citizenship.

Added to this, the spread of lawless attacks upon the negro, North, South and West—even in the Springfield made famous by Lincoln—often accompanied by revolting brutalities, sparing neither sex, nor age nor youth, could not but shock the author of the sentiment that "government of the people, by the people, for the people shall not perish from the earth."

Silence under these conditions means tacit approval. The indifference of the North is already responsible for more than one assault upon democracy, and every such attack reacts as unfavorably upon whites as upon blacks. Discrimination once permitted cannot be bridled; recent history in the South shows that in forging chains for the negroes, the white voters are forging chains for themselves. "A house divided against itself cannot stand"; this government cannot exist half slave and half free any better to-day than it could in 1861. Hence we call upon all the believers in democracy to join in a national conference for the discussion of present evils, the voicing of protests, and the renewal of the struggle for civil and political liberty.

Miss Jane Addams, Chicago

Ray Stannard Baker, New York

Mrs. Ida Wells-Barnett, Chicago

Mrs. Harriet Stanton Blatch, New York

Mr. Samuels Bowles *(Springfield Republican)*

Professor W. L. Bulkley, New York

Miss Kate Claghorn, New York

E. H. Clement, Boston

Professor John Dewey, New York

Miss Mary E. Dreier, Brooklyn

Professor W. E. B. Du Bois, Atlanta

Dr. John L. Elliott, New York

Mr. William Lloyd Garrison, Boston

Rev. Francis J. Grimke, Washington, D.C.

Professor Thomas C. Hall, New York

Rabbi Emil G. Hirsch, Chicago

Rev. John Haynes Holmes, New York

Hamilton Holt, New York

William Dean Howells, New York

Rev. Jerkin Lloyd Jones, Chicago

Mrs. Florence Kelley, New York

Rev. Walter Laidlaw, New York

Rev. Frederick Lynch, New York

Miss Helen Marot, New York

Miss Mary E. McDowell, Chicago

Prof. J. G. Merrill, Connecticut

Mr. John E. Milholland, New York

Dr. Henry Moskowitz, New York

Miss Leonora O'Reilly, New York

Miss Mary W. Ovington, New York

Rev. Charles H. Parkhurst, New York

Rev. John P. Peters, New York

J. G. Phelps-Stokes, New York

Louis F. Post, Chicago

Dr. Jane Robbins, New York

Charles Edward Russell, New York

William M. Salter, Chicago

Joseph Smith, Boston

Mrs. Anna Garlin Spencer, New York

Judge Wendell S. Stafford, Washington, D.C.

Lincoln Steffens, Boston

Miss Helen Stokes, New York

Mrs. Mary Church Terrell, Washington, D.C.

Professor W. I. Thomas, Chicago

President Charles F. Thwing, Western Reserve University

Oswald Garrison Villard, New York

Mrs. Henry Villard, New York

Miss Lillian D. Wald, New York

Dr. J. Milton Waldron, Washington, D.C.

William English Walling, New York

Bishop Alexander Walters, New York

Dr. William Ward, New York

Mrs. Rodman Wharton, Philadelphia

Miss Susan P. Wharton, Philadelphia

Horace White, New York

Mayor Brand Whitlock, Toledo

Rabbi Stephen S. Wise, New York

President Mary E. Wooley, Mt. Holyoke College

Rev. M. St. Croix Wright, New York

Professor Charles Zueblin, Boston

Major Officers of the NAACP, 1910–1936

Robert W. Bagnall	Director of Branches	1921–29
Lucille Black	Regional Field Secretary	1928–45
Frances Blascoer	Secretary	1910–11
Dr. W. E. B. Du Bois	Director of Publications & Research; Editor of *The Crisis*	1910–34
Charles Houston	Special Counsel	1935–39
Addie W. Hunton	Field Secretary	1921–24
James Weldon Johnson	Field Secretary	1916–20
	Acting Secretary	1920
	Secretary	1920–30
Daisy E. Lampkin	Regional Field Secretary	1930–38
Roual Freeman Nash	Secretary	1916–17
May Childs Nerney	Secretary	1912–16
Mary White Ovington	Secretary	1911–12
	Acting Secretary	1916
	Acting Chairman of the Board	1917–18
	Chairman of the Board	1919–32
	Treasurer	1933–47
William Pickens	Associate Field Secretary	1919
	Field Secretary	1920–38
Herbert J. Seligman	Director of Publicity	1922–32
John R. Shillady	Secretary	1918–20
Joel E. Spingarn	Chairman of the Board	1914–19
	Treasurer	1919–30
	President	1930–39
Dr. Louis T. Wright	Chairman of the Board	1935–52

Source: Minutes of Annual Reports, NAACP

1. Origins of the NAACP

1. Charles Flint Kellogg, *NAACP: A History of the National Association for the Advancement of Colored People, Volume I: 1909–1920* (Baltimore: Johns Hopkins University Press, 1967), chapter 1. There is little controversy or variation on the early days of the NAACP. For those wanting more detail than Kellogg, consult Minnie Finch, *The NAACP: Its Fight for Justice* (Metuchen, New Jersey and London: Scarecrow Press, 1981); Warren D. St. James, *NAACP: Triumphs of a Press Group, 1909–1980* (Smithtown, New York: Exposition Press, 1980); James McPherson, *The Abolitionist Legacy: From Reconstruction to the NAACP* (Princeton: Princeton University Press, 1975), especially Part Three, "The Revival of Militancy"; and Robert L. Zangrando, *The NAACP Crusade against Lynching, 1909–1950* (Philadelphia: Temple University Press, 1980), chapters 1 and 2.

2. McPherson, *The Abolitionist Legacy*, p. 370.

3. Proceedings of the National Negro Conference, New York, May 31 and June 1, 1909 (n.p., n.d.). Archives of the National Association for the Advancement of Colored People (Manuscript Division, Library of Congress); hereafter referred to as NAACP.

4. *New York Age*, June 10, 1909.

5. Louis R. Harlan, *Booker T. Washington: The Wizard of Tuskegee, 1901–1915* (New York: Oxford University Press, 1983), p. 359.

6. W. E. B. Du Bois, *The Amenia Conference: An Historic Gathering* (Amenia, New York: Troutbeck Press, 1925).

7. Kellogg, *NAACP*, p. 7.

8. August Meier and Elliot Rudwick, *Along the Color Line* (Urbana, Illinois: University of Illinois Press, 1976), pp. 94–127.

9. Zangrando, *Crusade against Lynching*, p. 27. Zangrando provides a thorough and complete treatment of the anti-lynching campaign and should be consulted by those who want a more extensive description of the NAACP's activities in this area.

10. Zangrando, chapter 3.

11. *The Crisis* 1 (November 1910), p. 14; *The Crisis* (December 1910), p. 26; NAACP, "The First Line of Defense: A Summary of 20 Years' Civil Rights Struggle for America's Negroes," pamphlet (New York, 1929).

12. *The Crisis* 1 (November 1910), p. 14; NAACP, "The First Line."

13. *The Crisis* 1 (March 1911), p. 15.

14. *Guinn v. United States*, 238 U.S. 347 (1915).

15. *Buchanan v. Warley*, 245 U.S. 60 (1917).

16. Kellogg, *NAACP*, pp. 184–85; *Buchanan*, p. 62.

17. *Moore v. Dempsey*, 261 U.S. 86 (1923).

18. Richard Kluger, *Simple Justice: The History of Brown v. Board of Education* (New York: Vintage, 1977), pp. 113–14.

19. *Corrigan v. Bulkley*, 271 U.S. 323 (1926).

20. *Nixon v. Herndon*, 273 U.S. 536 (1927).

21. *Harmon v. Taylor*, 273 U.S. 668 (1926); Kluger, *Simple Justice*, pp. 122, 137.

22. *City of Richmond v. Deans*, 37 F.2d 712 (1930).

23. *City of Richmond v. Deans*, 281 U.S. 704 (1930).

2. "The NAACP Comes of Age"

1. Some material in this chapter appeared in " 'The NAACP Comes of Age': The Defeat of Judge Parker," in *Developing Dixie: Modernization in a Traditional Society*, ed. Winfred B. Moore, Jr., et al. (New York: Greenwood Press, 1988), pp. 73–90; Walter White to Elliot Thurston, March 11, 1930, Archives of the NAACP, administrative file C-391.

2. Walter White to James A. Cobb, March 12, 1930, C-391; Elliot Thurston to Walter White, March 19, 1930, administrative file C-397.

3. "Associate Justice," presidential files, Herbert Hoover Papers, Hoover Institution Archives (Stanford, California); hereafter referred to as Hoover Institution Archives, Box 63. "Biographies of Men Considered," Herbert Hoover, Herbert Hoover Presidential Library (West Branch, Iowa); hereafter referred to as Hoover Library Papers.

4. Mabel Walker Willebrandt to Herbert Hoover, February 8, 1929, "Cabinet Appointments," campaign and transition file, Hoover Library Papers.

5. Harlan Fiske Stone to Herbert Hoover, unsigned memo, February 14, 1929, "Cabinet Appointments," Hoover Library Papers.

6. Judge John J. Parker, Member U.S. Circuit Court of Appeals, 4th Circuit, "Judiciary: Supreme Court of United States," Hoover Library Papers, p. 2.

7. For a fuller discussion of this lily-white strategy, see Richard B. Sherman, "Republicans and Negroes: The Lessons of Normalcy," *Phylon* 27 (Spring 1966): 63–79.

8. Donald J. Lislio, *Hoover, Blacks, and Lily Whites: A Study of Southern Strategies* (Chapel Hill: University of North Carolina Press, 1985), especially chapters 6 and 7.

9. William C. Burris, "John J. Parker and Supreme Court Policy: A Case Study in Judicial Control," Ph.D. diss., University of North Carolina, 1965, pp. 16–64; Judge John J. Parker, Hoover Library Papers.

10. Burris, pp. 16–64; C. Vann Woodward, *Origins of the New South: 1877–1913* (Baton Rouge: Louisiana State University Press, 1951), pp. 373–462.

11. *Charlotte Observer*, April 18, 1920.

12. Walter White, *A Man Called White: The Autobiography of Walter White* (Bloomington: Indiana University Press, 1948), p. 104.

13. "Report of the Acting Secretary" (for the April meeting of the

board, NAACP, 1930), p. 1; hereafter cited as "Secretary's Report." The author quoted from the NAACP's version, since this was the version sent out to the branches and used in speeches.

14. Dr. A. M. Riveria to Walter White, March 24, 1930, NAACP administrative file C-397.

15. "Secretary's Report" (for the April meeting of the board, 1930), p. 6.

16. "Secretary's Report," p. 2. The selected states were Arizona, California, Colorado, Delaware, Illinois, Indiana, Kansas, Kentucky, Maryland, Massachusetts, Michigan, Minnesota, Missouri, Montana, Nebraska, Nevada, New Jersey, New Mexico, New York, North Carolina, Ohio, Utah, Washington, Wisconsin, and West Virginia.

17. White, *A Man Called White*, pp. 105–106; "Secretary's Report" (for the April meeting of the board, 1930), p. 2.

18. *New York Times*, April 13, 1930; White, *A Man Called White*, p. 105.

19. "Secretary's Report" (for the April meeting of the board, 1930), p. 2.

20. *A Man Called White*, p. 106; "Confirmation of the Hon. John J. Parker to Be an Associate Justice of the Supreme Court of the United States," *Hearings before the Subcommittee on the Judiciary*, U.S. Senate, 71st Congress, 2nd Session, April 5, 1930 (Washington, D.C.: GPO, 1930), p. 74.

21. Walter White, "The Negro and the Supreme Court," *Harper's* 157 (January 1931): 239.

22. "Confirmation of the Hon. John J. Parker," *Hearings*, p. 80.

23. Irving Bernstein, *A History of the American Worker, 1920–1937: The Lean Years* (Cambridge, Massachusetts: The Riverside Press, 1960), pp. 89, 131.

24. "Confirmation of the Hon. John J. Parker," *Hearings*, pp. 77–79.

25. "Secretary's Report" (for the April meeting of the board, 1930), p. 2; "Minutes of the Meeting of the Board of Directors," NAACP, April 14, 1930, p. 1; hereafter cited as "Board Minutes."

26. Mrs. Minnie M. Scott, executive secretary, National Association of Colored Women, to Walter White, April 26, 1930, NAACP administrative file C-397.

27. Richard L. Watson, Jr., "The Defeat of Judge Parker: A Study in Pressure Groups and Politics," *Mississippi Valley Historical Review* 50 (September 1963): 220; Claudius O. Johnson, *Borah of Idaho* (Seattle: University of Washington Press, 1967), pp. 450–52.

28. White, *A Man Called White*, p. 106.

29. White, p. 108.

30. White, p. 108; *New York Times*, April 14, 1930, p. 6. J. E. Shephard was representative of Parker's black support. He was a leading educator in the South and ran a state school; his politics by necessity were accommodating.

31. J. E. Shephard to Lee Overman, March 29, 1930, Parker Papers (Southern Historical Collection, University of North Carolina), Personal Series, Box 5; hereafter cited as Parker Papers.

32. J. E. Shephard to Carl Murphy, April 5, 1930, Parker Papers, Box 5.

33. J. E. Shephard to John Parker, April 12, 1930, Parker Papers, Box 5. Shephard informed Parker that he was soliciting endorsements from Ohio, Indiana, Kentucky, Massachusetts, Illinois, New York, Maryland, West Virginia, and Missouri.

34. M. K. Tyson to John J. Parker, March 28, 1930, Parker Papers, Box 5.

35. M. K. Tyson to John J. Parker, May 7, 1930, Parker Papers, Box 5.

36. Associated Negro Press press release, "Plaindealer Supports Parker," May 5, 1930, Claude Albert Barnett Papers, 1919–1967, Parker file, Chicago State Historical Society, Chicago, Illinois; hereafter cited as A.N.P. Press Release.

37. *Baltimore Afro-American,* April 12, 1930, p. 1; White, *A Man Called White,* p. 108; A.N.P. Press Release, "Defeat of Judge Parker," May 14, 1930.

38. *Baltimore Afro-American,* May 17, 1930, p. 1.

39. Mary White Ovington, *The Walls Came Tumbling Down* (New York: Harcourt, Brace, and World, 1947), p. 255.

40. A.N.P. Press Release, "Press Association Official Protests Parker," May 5, 1930; White, "The Negro and the Supreme Court," *Harper's* 157 (January 1931): 240.

41. A.N.P. Press Release, "Parker Fight Shows Up Some Negro Friends," May 7, 1930.

42. *New York Times,* April 19, 1930, pp. 8, 20.

43. *New York Times,* April 17, 1930, p. 6; April 20, 1930, p. 11; April 21, 1930, p. 22; April 23, 1930, p. 2.

44. A separate file of letters involving Parker, Davis, and Blair is contained in Parker Papers, Personal Series, Box 6. Correspondence and memoranda are too numerous to detail except for the more important ones cited in the text.

45. Henry E. Davis to John J. Parker, April 16, 1930, Parker Papers, Box 6.

46. Thomas Guthrie to John J. Parker, April 16, 1930, Parker Papers, Box 6.

47. A. H. Vandenburg to R. K. Smothers, April 28, 1930 (copy), Parker Papers, Box 6.

48. Mount Vernon, new branch of NAACP to Robert F. Wagner, April 4, 1930, NAACP administrative file C-397.

49. Herbert Seligman to Walter White, May 1, 1930, administrative file C-39.

50. Congressional Record, 71st Congress, 2nd Session, 1930, pp. 7810, 7821, 8433–8435; Watson, "The Defeat of Judge Parker," pp.

224–30; *New York Times*, May 8, 1930, p. 8. The opposition to Parker appears to be a precursor to the New Deal coalition. This will be examined further in chapter 3.

51. Darlene Clark Hine, "The NAACP and the Supreme Court: Walter F. White and the Defeat of Judge John J. Parker, 1930," *Negro History Bulletin*, vol. 40, no. 5, 1977, p. 756. Hine notes that in the early years of the Association, the fight against injustice was almost always coupled with a fight to "institutionalize and sustain the National Association for the Advancement of Colored People."

52. B. Joyce Ross, *J. E. Spingarn and the Rise of the NAACP, 1911–1939* (New York: Atheneum, 1972), pp. 164–216; White, *A Man Called White*, p. 107.

53. "Report of Branches" (for the June meeting of the board of directors, 1930), NAACP, p. 7.

54. "Report of Branches," 1930, p. 7.

55. Daisy E. Lampkin to Robert Bagnall, April 17, 1930, NAACP administrative file C-67.

56. Daisy Lampkin to Walter White, April 24, 1930, NAACP administrative file C-67.

57. Walter White to Robert Bagnall, William Pickens, Daisy Lampkin, May 2, 1930, NAACP administrative file C-67.

58. Daisy Lampkin to Walter White, April 24, 1930, NAACP administrative file C-67.

59. *Amsterdam News* (New York), April 23, 1930, p. 1.

60. Herbert J. Seligman, "The NAACP Battle Front," *The Crisis* 38, 6 (1931), p. 197.

61. References to the Parker fight were used as a reason for support as late as 1934. See Mary White Ovington, "The Year of Jubilee," *The Crisis* 41 (1934), p. 7.

62. Du Bois, "The Defeat of John J. Parker," pp. 225–27, 248.

63. *Twentieth NAACP Annual Report* (1929), p. 48; *Twenty-First NAACP Annual Report* (1930), p. 45; *Twenty-Second NAACP Annual Report* (1931), p. 38; *Twenty-Third NAACP Annual Report* (1932), p. 23.

64. Heywood Broun, "The Black Voter," *The Crisis* 38, 11 (November 1930), p. 369.

65. William Griffin, "Black Insurgency in the Republican Party of Ohio, 1920–1932," *Ohio History* 82 (Winter–Spring 1932), pp. 24–45; Sherman, "Republicans and Negroes," pp. 63–79.

66. William H. Hastie, "A Look at the NAACP," *The Crisis* 46, 9 (September 1939), pp. 236–64, 274.

67. The motto was printed on official NAACP stationery in 1930. Examples can be found in Daisy Lampkin's correspondence for May, June, and July, 1930, NAACP administrative file C-67.

3. The Parker Fight

1. For example, see Nancy J. Weiss, *Farewell to the Party of Lincoln: Blacks in the Age of FDR* (Princeton: Princeton University Press, 1983),

p. 17; Harvard Sitkoff, *A New Deal for Blacks: The Emergence of Civil Rights as a National Issue* (New York: Oxford University Press, 1978), pp. 85–86; and Bernstein, *A History of the American Worker,* pp. 195–202. Weiss writes that "Wagner had been the only Senator to raise the issue of Parker's alleged racial bias," clearly downplaying the importance of race to the final vote. Sitkoff concludes, "In May [1930], for the first time since 1894, the Senate rejected a presidential recommendation for the Supreme Court. Negro leaders shouted their joy. . . . Actually, blacks had little to do with the decision." Following in this vein, Bernstein also noted that "Parker denied that he had advocated in 1920 that Negroes should not be permitted the suffrage. . . . The main task of the supporters of the nomination was to explain away the Red Jacket decision," not his statements on race. See also Watson, "The Defeat of Judge Parker"; and William C. Burris, "The Senate Rejects a Judge: A Study of the John J. Parker Case" (unpublished) 361, Political Studies Program Research Report No. 3 (Chapel Hill: Department of Political Science, University of North Carolina, 1962). Both authors downplay the role of race in Parker's defeat, although they do differ on the role of labor. Watson is much more impressed with the efforts of the AFL.

2. Zangrando, *The NAACP Crusade against Lynching,* chapters 1–4.

3. *Congressional Record,* 71st Congress, 2d sess., 1930, pp. 6473, 6569, 6579.

4. Ibid., p. 7001.

5. Ibid., p. 7273.

6. Ibid., p. 7793.

7. Ibid., pp. 7811–13, 7819, 7822, 7888.

8. Ibid., pp. 7822, 7930, 7932–35.

9. Bernstein, *History of the American Worker,* pp. 195–202.

10. *Congressional Record,* 71st Congress, 2d sess., pp. 7941–42.

11. Ibid., pp. 7943.

12. Ibid., pp. 8033–37.

13. Paul L. Murphy, *The Constitution in Crisis, 1918–1969* (New York: Harper and Row, 1972), pp. 101–102; Henry J. Abraham, *Justice and Presidents: A Political History of Appointments to the Supreme Court,* 2d ed. (New York: Oxford University Press, 1985), pp. 198–200.

14. *Congressional Record,* 71st Congress, 2d sess., p. 8038.

15. Ibid.

16. "Perry Howard Case Opened Monday," *Periscope* 8, December 1928, A.N.P.; "Perry Howard to Face Second Trial," March 15, 1929, A.N.P.

17. Robert Moton to Herbert Hoover, February 5, 1930, "Race Discrimination, 1929–1930," presidential file, Hoover Institution Archives, Box 79.

18. Arthur S. Link, "What Happened to the Progressive Movement in the 1920s?" *American Historical Review* 64, no. 4 (July 1959), pp. 833–51.

19. *Congressional Record,* 71st Congress, 2d sess., pp. 8040–42, 8116.

20. Ibid., p. 8337.
21. Ibid., p. 8358.
22. Ibid., p. 8435.
23. Ibid., pp. 8432–33.
24. Ibid., pp. 8444, 8449.
25. Ibid., p. 8476.
26. Robert E. Burke, ed., "Johnson to My Dear Boys, May 3, 1930," *The Diary and Letters of Hiram Johnson, 1922–33*, vol. 5 (New York: Garland Publishing, Inc. 1983), p. 2.
27. *Congressional Record*, 71st Congress, 2d sess., p. 8567.
28. Lislio, *Hoover and the Lily-Whites*, p. 232. Lislio cites an event at the annual American Bankers Convention of 1930, where Hoover told a delegate that "Judge Parker's rejection is an outrage. I don't know what the country is coming to if things are to be run by demagogue and Negro politicians."
29. *Atlanta Constitution*, May 8, 1930.
30. *New York Times*, May 8, 1930; a partial listing of citations on this issue includes *Congressional Record*, 71st Congress, 2d sess., p. 8037–38, 8116.
31. *Atlanta Constitution*, May 8, 1930.
32. Memorandum entitled "The Department of Justice Has Prepared the Following Memorandum on the Opinion of Circuit Judge John J. Parker in International Organization, UMW of America v. Red Jacket Consolidated Coal and Coke Co.," 18F (2d) 893, "Judge John Parker," personal file, Hoover Library Papers.
33. *New York Times*, May 8, 1930; a partial listing of citations on this issue includes *Congressional Record*, 71st Congress, 2d sess., pp. 7273, 7822, 7930, 7932, 8034, 8038, 8476.
34. *New York Times*, May 8, 1930; a partial listing of citations on this issue includes *Congressional Record*, 71st Congress, 2d sess., pp. 8033–34, 8040, 8110, 8116, 8192, 8476.
35. Arthur S. Link, *Woodrow Wilson and the Progressive Era, 1910–1917* (New York: Harper and Row, 1954), pp. 13–16; David Burner, *The Politics of Provincialism: The Democratic Party in Transition 1918–1932* (New York: W. W. Norton and Company, 1967), pp. 163–67.
36. V. O. Key, *The Responsible Electorate: Rationality in Presidential Voting* (Cambridge, Massachusetts: Harvard University Press, 1966), p. 33.
37. James Boyland, *The New Deal Coalition and the Election of 1948* (New York: Garland Publishing, Inc., 1981), p. 2.

4. Long Memories

1. "Report of Branches" (for the June meeting of the board of directors, NAACP, 1930), p. 3.
2. W. E. B. Du Bois, "The Defeat of Judge Parker," *The Crisis* 37 (1930), p. 225; White, *A Man Called White*, p. 111.

3. Meier and Rudwick, *Along the Color Line,* p. 115.

4. Francis Broderick, *W. E. B. Du Bois: Negro Leader in Time of Crisis* (Stanford: Stanford University Press, 1959), pp. 150–79; Elliot Rudwick, "W. E. B. Du Bois in the Role of *Crisis* Editor," *Journal of Negro History* 43 (July 1958), pp. 214–40.

5. Broderick, *Du Bois,* pp. 150–79; Rudwick, "Du Bois," pp. 214–40; Elliot Rudwick, *W. E. B. Du Bois: Propagandist of the Negro Protest* (New York: Atheneum Press, 1968), chapter 10.

6. *Twentieth Annual Report of the NAACP* (1929).

7. "NAACP Board Minutes," July 14, 1930, pp. 6–7.

8. William Pickens, "Aftermath of Anti-Parker Fight," Associated Negro Press, Deadline Release 5, May 14, 1930.

9. Kelly Miller to Walter White, November 13, 1930, NAACP; White, *A Man Called White,* p. 111.

10. "NAACP Board Minutes," January 5, 1931, p. 3; April 13, 1931, p. 4.

11. "NAACP Board Minutes," March 9, 1931, p. 5.

12. Walter White to branches, May 8, 1930; NAACP branch files G-224.

13. Robert Bagnall to branches, May 22, 1930; NAACP branch files G-224.

14. "Washington Tells Walter White Negro Star Is in Ascendant," May 23, 1930, Press Service of the National Association for the Advancement of Colored People, Publicity File C-398; hereafter cited as NAACP Press Release.

15. *Baltimore Afro-American,* April 26, 1930, p. 6.

16. *Pittsburgh Courier,* October 11, 1930, p. 10; *Chicago Defender,* May 10, 1930, p. 14.

17. Du Bois, *The Defeat of Judge Parker,* p. 225. The following is the entire list of candidates as printed in Du Bois's article with their eventual disposition and type of campaign run against them added by the author:

FALL OF 1930

major campaign:	Allen of Kansas [defeated]
	Baird of New Jersey [retired from Senate; ran for governor of New Jersey, 1931, defeated]
	McCulloch of Ohio [defeated]
minor publicity campaign:	Gillette of Massachusetts [won]
	Hastings of Delaware [won]
very minor campaign:	Grundy of Pennsylvania [defeated]
no campaign:	Goff of West Virginia [did not run]

FALL OF 1932

major campaign:	Watson of Indiana [defeated]
major publicity campaign:	Shortridge of California [defeated]
no campaign:	Bingham of Connecticut [did not run]

FALL OF 1934
major publicity campaign: Kean of New Jersey [defeated]
                                Fess of Ohio [defeated]
                                Hatfield of West Virginia [defeated]
                                Patterson of Missouri [defeated]
                                Reed of Pennsylvania [defeated]
                                Townsend of Delaware [defeated]
no campaign: Goldsborough of Maryland [did not run]

18. "Report of the Acting Secretary" (for the June meeting of the board of directors), NAACP, 1930, pp. 3–4.

19. "'Parker Victory Helped Get Members,' Says Kansas City NAACP," July 13, 1930, NAACP Press Release, administrative file C-398.

20. Undated list of prominent black ministers, lawyers, and others to be contacted in Kansas, subject file C-393.

21. Robert Bagnall to Dr. F. O. Miller, July 9, 1930, branch file G-74.

22. "Take Your Choice," undated administrative file C-393.

23. Roy Wilkins to Walter White, July 1, 1930, subject file C-393.

24. William Pickens, "The Negro Voter and Allen," *The Crisis* 36, 8 (1930), p. 338.

25. Roy Wilkins, *Standing Fast* (New York: Viking Press, 1982), pp. 98–99, 111.

26. "Senator George McGill Addresses Kansas State NAACP Meeting," Press Release, May 15, 1931, NAACP branch file G-70.

27. "NAACP Board Minutes," July 14, 1930, p. 6; memorandum to the board of directors from Mr. Bagnall, July 16, 1930, NAACP branch file G-151. For an earlier history of the conferences, see Kellogg, *NAACP*, pp. 134–36, 202.

28. Leslie J. Stegh, "A Paradox of Prohibition: Election of Robert J. Bulkley as Senator from Ohio, 1930," *Ohio History* 83 (Summer 1974), pp. 177, 181.

29. James Wilson to Thomas Donnelly, May 21, 1930; Thomas Donnelly to William Green, May 23, 1930; William Green to Thomas Donnelly, May 28, 1930. Papers of William Green, 1891–1952, AFL-CIO Archives, Washington, D.C., Box 2, Folder 68, Microfilm 13, #7.

30. Robert Bagnall to Mrs. K. T. Thompson, secretary, Alliance Branch, July 3, 1930, NAACP branch file G-151. This was a form letter which was sent to every branch in the state on name and address changes. Bagnall had written to the branches in Ohio inviting them to a state conference and explaining the conference structure. The conference was to facilitate communication between the branches and the national office.

31. Memorandum to the board of directors from Mr. Bagnall, July 14, 1930, NAACP branch file G-151.

32. Robert Bagnall to Mr. H. B. Shipp, July 17, 1930, NAACP branch file G-151; prototype of letter sent out to invitees.

33. Robert Bagnall to C. E. Dickinson, July 23, 1930, NAACP branch file G-151.

34. Ohio State Conference Minutes, July 29–30, 1930, pp. 1–3, NAACP branch file G-151.

35. Walter White to Elliot Thurston, September 4, 1930, NAACP administrative file C-395.

36. Memorandum from White's secretary to Walter White summarizing White's correspondence on this issue, including Thurston's reply. Inexplicably, the memorandum is dated September 3, 1930, a day before White wrote to Thurston. NAACP administrative file C-395.

37. "NAACP Board Minutes," September 8, 1930, p. 4; "Secretary's Report" (for the October meeting of the board of directors, NAACP), 1930, p. 1; and ibid. (for the November meeting of the board of directors, NAACP), 1930, p. 1.

38. "NAACP Board Minutes," September 8, 1930, p. 4.

39. "Report of a trip to Cleveland, September 19, 20, and 21 . . ." September 22, 1930, NAACP administrative file C-395.

40. C. E. Dickinson to Walter White, September 24, 1930, NAACP branch file G-151.

41. "Minutes of the Second Conference of the Ohio Branches. . . ," October 5, 1930, p. 1, NAACP branch file G-151.

42. "NAACP Board Minutes," October 5, 1930, p. 1.

43. Memorandum from national office to Ohio branches, October 6, 1930, NAACP administrative file C-395.

44. White, *A Man Called White*, pp. 112–13.

45. Miss Geraldyn R. Freeland to Walter White, November 4, 1930, NAACP branch file G-151.

46. NAACP, *Twenty-First Annual Report* (New York: 1931), p. 16.

47. Walter White to W. W. McDowell, Democratic State Central Committee, Montana, October 7, 1930, NAACP administrative file C-395.

48. "Victorious Candidates of Both Parties Thank NAACP for Aid," November 24, 1930, Press Release, NAACP branch file G-60.

49. C. C. Galloway to Walter White, July 27, 1930; William Pickens to C. C. Galloway, August 6, NAACP administrative file C-391.

50. "Slapping Our Political Enemies and Supporting Our Friends," *Louisville News*, September 12, 1930.

51. "New Jersey State Conference Opposes Baird for Governor," Press Release, March 6, 1931, NAACP administrative file C-393.

52. Minutes of the board of directors, May 11, 1931, p. 5.

53. "Why the NAACP Is Opposing Baird in New Jersey," August 21, 1931, administrative file C-393.

54. "The NAACP Appeals to You" (no date), NAACP administrative file C-393.

55. "New Jersey Branch Challenges Baird to Debate with Walter White," October 13, 1930, administrative file C-393; Walter White to offices of New Jersey branches of NAACP, October 21, 1930, NAACP administrative file C-34.

56. L. F. Coles to Walter White, October 21, 1931, NAACP administrative file C-34.

57. Walter White to Herbert Seligman, November 5, 1931, NAACP administrative file C-34.

58. Mrs. F. K. Bailey to Robert Bagnall, September 10, 1930, NAACP branch file G-60.

59. "Lynch Law: America's Grave Problem. . . ," October 30, 1930, Press Release, NAACP branch file G-60.

60. Robert Bagnall to Walter White, September 7, 1932, NAACP branch file G-60.

61. Robert Bagnall to Mrs. F. K. Bailey, September 10, 1932, NAACP branch file G-60.

62. Mrs. F. K. Bailey to Walter White, September 8, 1932; Walter White to Mrs. F. K. Bailey, September 18, 1932, NAACP branch file G-60.

63. "Pro-Parker Senator on Spot. . . ," *Pittsburgh Courier,* October 10, 1932, NAACP branch file G-60.

64. Robert Bagnall to Walter White, November 4, 1932, NAACP branch file G-64.

65. "Greatest Negro Political Revolts," October 17, 1932, Press Release, NAACP branch file G-60.

66. Mrs. F. K. Bailey to Walter White, November 10, 1932, NAACP branch file G-60.

67. Robert Bagnall to Mrs. F. K. Bailey, November 14, 1932, NAACP branch file G-60.

68. Robert L. Bailey to Walter White, November 11, 1932, NAACP branch file G 60.

69. Robert L. Bailey to Walter White, November 11, 1932, NAACP branch file G-60.

70. Mrs. F. K. (Katherine) Bailey to Walter White, April 22, 1936, NAACP branch file G-60.

71. Telegram from Walter White to Mrs. Katherine Bailey, April 22, 1936, NAACP branch file G-60.

72. "Indiana State Conference of Branches Sends Questionnaires to Candidates to State Legislature. . . ," Press Release, April 30, 1936, NAACP branch file G-60.

73. St. Paul, Minnesota *News,* May 29, 1932, NAACP administrative file C-391.

74. "Finish of the Parker Fight," *The Crisis* 40, 12 (1934), p. 364.

5. An Assessment of the Parker Fight

1. White, *A Man Called White,* p. 114.

2. Dr. Frank P. Graham to Mr. Marvin McIntyre, secretary to President Roosevelt, October 8, 1942. President's personnel file, papers of Franklin Delano Roosevelt, Franklin Delano Roosevelt Presidential Library, Hyde Park, New York.

3. "John J. Parker: Senior Circuit Judge: Fourth Circuit," *American Bar Association Journal* 32 (December 1946) pp. 857–58.

4. Watson, "The Defeat of Judge Parker," p. 234.

5. *Congressional Record,* 71st Congress, 2d sess., 1930, p. 7793.

6. John J. Parker to Horace Williams, April 7, 1930, Parker Papers, Box 5.

7. Burris, "John J. Parker and Supreme Court Policy," pp. 78–87.

8. Some examples of property rights cases considered by Parker were *Kelleher v. French,* 22 F.2d 341 (1927); *Ferris v. Wilbur,* 27 F.2d 262 (1928); and *United States v. Taylor,* 33 F.2d 724 (1929); for a statement on his continuing to follow precedent even though he disagreed, see John J. Parker to Ernst F. Cochran, June 16, 1927, Parker Papers, Box 17.

9. "John J. Parker: Senior Circuit Judge," p. 856.

10. *Campbell v. Alleghany,* 75 F.2d 947 (1935).

11. *Bradford v. Fahey,* 76 F.2d 628 (1935).

12. *Louisville Bank v. Radford,* 74 295 U.S. 555 (1935).

13. *Barnette v. West Virginia State Board of Education,* 47 F. Supp. 251 (1942).

14. *Barnette,* p. 253.

15. *Frankfeld v. U.S.,* 198 F.2d (1952); *Scales v. U.S.,* 227 F.2d 581 (1955).

16. *Alston v. Norfolk School Bd.,* 112 F.2d 992 (1940).

17. White, *A Man Called White,* p. 114; Gilbert Ware, *William Hastie: Grace under Pressure* (New York: Oxford University Press, 1984), p. 64.

18. *Alston,* p. 992.

19. *Brotherhood of Locomotive Firemen and Enginemen et al. v. Tunstall,* 163 F.2d 289 (1947).

20. *Brotherhood* (1947); Genna Rae McNeil, *Groundwork: Charles Hamilton Houston and the Struggle for Civil Rights* (Philadelphia: University of Pennsylvania Press, 1983), pp. 161–62.

21. *Tunstall v. Brotherhood of Locomotive Firemen and Enginemen et al.* 323 U.S. 199, 201–204, 207, 210–14 (1944). Several cases had been made companion cases.

22. *Rice v. Elmore,* 165 F.2d 387 (1947).

23. *Rice,* p. 392.

24. *Baskin v. Brown,* 174 F.2d 391 (1949).

25. *Baskin,* p. 394.

26. *Briggs v. Elliot,* 98 F. Supp. 529 (1951); Daniel M. Rice, "Judge John J. Parker's Legal Career: Stimulus for Change or Conservator for the Status Quo," senior independent study, history, College of Wooster, 1985.

27. *Briggs,* p. 536; Richard Kluger, *Simple Justice: The History of Brown v. Board of Education,* (New York: Vintage Books, 1977), pp. 315–21.

28. Kluger, *Simple Justice,* p. 332.

29. *Briggs,* p. 532.

30. Ibid., pp. 547–48.

31. Walter A. Huxman to John J. Parker, June 25, 1951, Parker Papers, Box 38.

32. *Sweatt v. Painter*, 339 U.S. 629 (1950); *McLaurin v. Oklahoma State Regents for Higher Education*, 389 U.S. 637 (1950).

33. *Brown v. Board of Education of Topeka, Kansas*, 98 F. Supp. 797 (1951); *Belton v. Gebhart* and *Bulah v. Gebhart*, 32 Del. Ch. 343, 87A 2d 862; *Bolling v. Sharpe*, 347 U.S. 497 (1954); *Davis v. County School Board of Prince Edward County*, 103 F. Supp. 337 (1952).

34. Kluger, *Simple Justice*, pp. 652–56.

35. *Brown v. Board of Education*, 347 U.S. 483 (1954).

36. *Brown v. Board of Education*, 349 U.S. 294 (1955).

37. *Briggs v. Elliot*, 132 F. Supp. 776 (1955), p. 779.

38. Kluger, *Simple Justice*, p. 751.

39. Jack Bass, *Unlikely Heroes* (New York: Touchstone Books, 1981), p. 298.

40. Burris, "John J. Parker," p. 250.

41. Ibid., p. 208.

42. Simon Sobeloff to John J. Parker, June 25, 1957, Parker Papers, Box 46.

43. *School Board of City of Newport News v. Atkins*, 246 F.2d 325 (1957).

44. *Briggs 1*, p. 529.

45. *Charlotte Observer*, February 22, 1910; May 19, 1929.

46. John J. Parker to Warren G. Harding, June 6, 1922, Parker Papers, Box 2, Folder 24.

47. John J. Parker to H. F. Seawell, February 19, 1925, Parker Papers, Box 2, Folder 28.

48. John J. Parker to Rush Holland, June 26, 1925, Parker Papers, Box 2, Folder 28.

49. Parker to Holland, Parker Papers.

50. John J. Parker to Samuel I. Parker, July 7, 1925, Parker Papers, Box 2, Folder 32.

51. John J. Parker to Lee Overman, August 18, 1925, Parker Papers, Box 2, Folder 26; John J. Parker to Furnifold Simmons, August 18, 1925, Parker Papers, Box 2, Folder 36.

52. John J. Parker to David H. Blair, April 3, 1930, Parker Papers.

53. *New York Times*, April 21, 1930.

54. Thomas W. Davis to David H. Blair, April 13 and 14, 1930; Kenneth Royall to John J. Parker, April 17, 1930; John J. Parker to Thomas W. Davis, April 24, 1930; Edwin Y. Webb to Parker, April 11, 1930, April 12, 1930; John J. Parker to Webb, April 19, 1930, Parker Papers.

55. *Washington Post*, May 18, 1930; Robert G. Taylor to John J. Parker, April 30, 1930, Parker Papers.

56. *New York Times*, May 8, 1930.

57. John J. Parker to Harlan Fiske Stone, January 10, 1925, Parker Papers, Box 2, Folder 26.

58. John J. Parker to Horace Williams, May 26, 1930, Parker Papers, Box 7, Folder 133.

59. John J. Parker to Samuel I. Parker, May 24, 1930, Parker Papers, Box 7, Folder 127.

60. I have noted just one letter of endorsement in these instances, although there were several in each case. Frank Graham to Franklin Delano Roosevelt, January 31, 1941, Papers of Franklin Delano Roosevelt, Franklin Delano Roosevelt Presidential Library, Hyde Park, New York; Robert G. Taylor to Harry S. Truman, September 11, 1945, Papers of Harry S. Truman, General File, Harry S. Truman Presidential Library, Independence, Missouri; Frank Graham to Harry S. Truman, July 27, 1949; S. W. Cramer to Dwight D. Eisenhower, December 31, 1953, Papers of Dwight David Eisenhower, Dwight David Eisenhower Presidential Library, Abilene, Kansas.

61. Every presidential library (from Hoover's to Eisenhower's) contained numerous materials from Parker. The number is truly voluminous and would not bear citing. An interesting characteristic is that the correspondence, except for discussion of appointments to two Nuremberg trials and some New Deal and World War II agencies, is all one-sided, from Parker to the presidents. The materials are in the Parker Papers also.

62. John J. Parker to the Honorable Henry J. Allen, May 26, 1930, Parker Papers, Folder 133.

Epilogue

1. For example, see Nancy J. Weiss, *Farewell to the Party of Lincoln: Blacks in the Age of FDR* (Princeton: Princeton University Press, 1983), chapter 4; Harvard Sitkoff, *A New Deal for Blacks: The Emergence of Civil Rights as a National Issue* (New York: Oxford University Press, 1978), chapter 4.

2. Mark Levy and Michael Kramer, *The Ethnic Factor* (New York: Simon and Schuster, 1973), p. 49; Vernon E. Jordan, Jr., "Blacks Have a Claim on Carter," *Newsweek*, November 22, 1976, p. 13.

3. Bernard Schwartz, *Super Chief: Earl Warren and His Supreme Court: A Judicial Biography* (New York: New York University Press, 1983), chapter 16.

4. *Time*, September 26, 1969, pp. 21–22; *Newsweek*, September 26, 1969, p. 36. For a discussion of both the Haynesworth and Carswell defeats, see Daryl Paulson, "The Senate Rejection of the Haynesworth and Carswell Nominations to the United States Supreme Court" (unpublished manuscript), presented at the fourth Citadel Conference of the South, Charleston, South Carolina, 1985.

5. *New York Times*, January 23, 1970.

6. *Congressional Quarterly*, April 10, 1970, pp. 943–46.

7. Nadine Cohodas, "For Robert Bork, the Real Test Begins Now," *Congressional Quarterly Weekly Report* 45 (September 12, 1987), pp. 2167–68.

8. Nadine Cohodas with Jacqueline Calmes, "White House in Desperate Struggle to Save Bork," *Congressional Quarterly Weekly Report* 45 (October 3, 1987), pp. 2366–69; Nathaniel Nash, "Bork Is Losing Southern Democrats while Picking up GOP Moderates," *New York Times*, September 27, 1987, p. 12.

9. *New York Times*, October 24, 1987.

BIBLIOGRAPHY

Manuscripts

Barnett, Claude Albert. Papers, 1919–1967. Chicago State Historical Society. Chicago, Illinois.

Burris, William C. "John J. Parker and Supreme Court Policy: A Case Study in Judicial Control." Ph.D. diss. University of North Carolina at Chapel Hill. 1965.

Eisenhower, Dwight David. Papers. Dwight David Eisenhower Presidential Library. Abilene, Kansas.

Hoover, Herbert. Papers. Herbert Hoover Archives. The Herbert Hoover Institution. Stanford University. Stanford, California.

Hoover, Herbert. Papers. Herbert Hoover Presidential Library. West Branch, Iowa.

National Association for the Advancement of Colored People. Files. National Office. New York City.

National Association for the Advancement of Colored People. Papers. Library of Congress. Washington, D.C.

Parker, John J. Papers. Southern Historical Collection. Wilson Library. The University of North Carolina at Chapel Hill. Chapel Hill, North Carolina.

Paulson, Daryl. "The Senate Rejection of the Haynesworth and Carswell Nominations to the United States Supreme Court." Unpublished manuscript. Presented at the Fourth Citadel Conference on the South. Charleston, South Carolina, 1985.

Rice, Daniel M. "Judge John J. Parker's Legal Career: Stimulus for Change or Conservation for the Status Quo." Senior Independent Study Project. College of Wooster. 1985.

Roosevelt, Franklin Delano. Papers. Franklin Delano Roosevelt Presidential Library. Hyde Park, New York.

Tillman, Nathaniel Patrick. "Walter Francis White: A Study in Interest Group Leadership." Ph.D. diss. University of Wisconsin, Madison. 1961.

Truman, Harry S. Papers. Harry S. Truman Presidential Library. Independence, Missouri.

Printed Materials

American Bar Association. "John J. Parker: Senior Circuit Judge: Fourth Circuit." *American Bar Association Journal* 32 (December 1946): 857–58.

Bass, Jack. *Unlikely Heroes.* New York: Touchstone Books, 1981.

Bernstein, Irving. *A History of the American Worker, 1920–1937: The Lean Years.* Cambridge, Massachusetts: The Riverside Press, 1960.

Boyland, James. *The New Deal Coalition and the Election of 1946.* New York: Garland Publishing, Inc. 1981.

Broderick, Francis. W. E. B. *Du Bois: Negro Leader in Time of Crisis.* Stanford: Stanford University Press, 1959.

Broun, Heywood. "The Black Voter." *The Crisis* 37 (1930): 369.

Burke, Robert E., ed. *The Diary and Letters of Hiram Johnson, 1922– 1933.* Vol. 5. New York: Garland Publishing, Inc., 1983.

Burner, David. *Herbert Hoover: A Public Life.* New York: Atheneum, 1984.

———. *The Politics of Provincialism: The Democratic Party in Transition.* New York: W. W. Norton and Company, 1967.

Cohodas, Nadine. "For Bork, the Real Test Begins Now." *Congressional Quarterly Weekly Report* 45 (September 12): 2159–77. Washington, D.C.: Congressional Quarterly, 1987.

Cohodas, Nadine, with Jacqueline Calmes. "White House in Desperate Struggle to Save Bork." *Congressional Quarterly Weekly Report* 45 (October 3): 2366–69.

Congress. *Congressional Record.* 71st Cong. Senate. 2d Session. Washington, D.C.: GPO, 1930.

Congress. *Congressional Record.* 71st Cong. Senate. 2d Session, Hearings before the Subcommittee of the Committee on the Judiciary. Washington, D.C.: GPO, 1930.

Du Bois, W. E. B. *The Amenia Conference: An Historic Gathering* Amenia, New York: Troutbeck Press, 1925.

———. "The Defeat of Judge Parker." *The Crisis* 37 (1930): 225–27, 248.

Finch, Minnie. *The NAACP: Its Fight for Justice.* Metuchen, New Jersey and London: Scarecrow Press, 1981.

Harlan, Louis R. *Booker T. Washington: The Wizard of Tuskegee, 1901– 1915* New York. Oxford University Press, 1983.

Hastie, William. "A Look at the NAACP." *The Crisis* 46 (1939): 263– 64, 274.

Hine, Darlene Clark. *Black Victory: The Rise and Fall of the White Primary in Texas.* Millwood, New York: KTO Press, 1979.

———. "The NAACP and the Supreme Court: Walter F. White and the Defeat of Judge John J. Parker, 1930." *Negro History Bulletin* 40, no. 5: 753–57.

Johnson, Claudius O. *Borah of Idaho.* Seattle: University of Washington Press, 1967.

Kellogg, Charles Flint. *NAACP: A History of the National Association for the Advancement of Colored People, Volume 1: 1909–1920.* Baltimore: Johns Hopkins University Press, 1967.

Key, V. O. *The Responsible Electorate: Rationality in Presidential Voting.* Cambridge, Massachusetts: Harvard University Press, 1966.

Kluger, Richard. *Simple Justice: The History of Brown v. Board of Education.* New York: Vintage, 1977.

Levy, Mark, and Michael Kramer. *The Ethnic Factor.* New York: Simon and Schuster, 1973.

Link, Arthur S. "What Happened to the Progressive Movement in the 1920s?" *American Historical Review* 64, no. 4 (July 1959): 833–51.

———. *Woodrow Wilson and the Progressive Era, 1910–1917.* New York: Harper and Row, 1954.

Lislio, Donald J. *Hoover, Blacks, and Lily Whites: A Study of Southern Strategies.* Chapel Hill: University of North Carolina Press, 1985.

McAdams, Doug. *Political Process and the Development of Black Insurgency, 1930–1970.* Chicago: University of Chicago Press, 1982.

McNeil, Genna Rae. *Groundwork: Charles Houston and the Struggle for Civil Rights.* Philadelphia: University of Pennsylvania Press, 1983.

McPherson, James. *The Abolitionist Legacy: From Reconstruction to the NAACP.* Princeton: Princeton University Press, 1975.

Meier, August, and Elliot Rudwick. *Along the Color Line.* Urbana, Illinois: University of Illinois Press, 1976.

National Association for the Advancement of Colored People. Annual Reports, 1911–1940.

———. *Thirty Years of Lynching in the United States, 1889–1919.* New York: NAACP, 1919.

———. *A Ten Year Fight against Lynching.* New York: NAACP, 1920.

———. *Notes on Lynching in the United States.* New York: NAACP, 1912.

———. "The First Line of Defense: A Summary of 20 Years' Civil Rights Struggle for America's Negroes." Pamphlet. New York: NAACP, 1929.

National Negro Conference. *Proceedings.* New York, 1909.

Ovington, Mary White. *The Walls Came Tumbling Down.* New York: Harcourt, Brace, and World, 1947.

———. "The Year of Jubilee." *The Crisis* 41 (1934): 7.

Pickens, William. "The Negro Voter and Allen." *The Crisis* 37 (1930): 338.

Ploski, Harry A., and Warren Marr, II, eds. *The Afro-Americans.* New York: The Bellwether Co., 1976.

Ross, B. Joyce. *J. E. Spingarn and the Rise of the NAACP, 1911–1939.* New York: Atheneum, 1972.

Rudwick, Elliot, *W. E. B. Du Bois: Propagandist of the Negro Protest.* New York: Atheneum Press, 1968.

———. "W. E. B. Du Bois in the Role of Crisis Editor." *Journal of Negro History* 43 (July 1958): 214–40.

St. James, Warren D. *NAACP: Triumphs of a Press Group, 1909–1980.* Smithtown, New York: Exposition Press, 1980.

Schwartz, Bernard. *Super Chief: Earl Warren and His Supreme Court: A Judicial Biography.* New York: New York University Press, 1983.

Seligman, Herbert J. "The NAACP Battle Front." *The Crisis* 38 (1931): 197.

Sherman, Richard B. "Republicans and Negroes: The Lessons of Normalcy." *Phylon* 27 (Spring 1966): 63–79.

Sitkoff, Harvard. *A New Deal for Blacks: The Emergence of Civil Rights as a National Issue.* New York: Oxford University Press, 1978.

Stegh, Leslie J. "A Paradox of Prohibition: Election of Robert J. Bulkley as Senator from Ohio, 1930." *Ohio History* 83 (1974): 170–82.

Tushnett, Mark V. *The NAACP's Legal Strategy against Segregated Education, 1925–1950.* Chapel Hill: The University of North Carolina Press, 1987.

Ware, Gilbert. *William Hastie: Grace under Pressure.* New York: Oxford University Press, 1984.

Watson, Richard L., Jr. "The Defeat of Judge Parker: A Study in Pressure Groups and Politics." *Mississippi Valley Historical Review* 50 (September 1963): 213–14.

Weiss, Nancy J. *Farewell to the Party of Lincoln: Blacks in the Age of FDR.* Princeton: Princeton University Press, 1983.

White, Walter. *A Man Called White: The Autobiography of Walter White.* Bloomington: Indiana University Press, 1970.

———. "The Negro and the Supreme Court." *Harpers* 157 (January 1931): 239.

———. "The Test of Ohio." *The Crisis* 36 (1930): 373–74.

Wilkins, Roy. *Standing Fast: The Autobiography of Roy Wilkins.* New York: Viking Press, 1982.

Woodward, C. Vann. *Origins of the New South: 1877–1913.* Baton Rouge: Louisiana State University Press, 1951.

Zangrando, Robert L. *The NAACP Crusade against Lynching, 1909–1950.* Philadelphia: Temple University Press, 1980.

Supreme Court Cases

Bolling v. Sharps, 347 U.S. 497 (1954).

Brown v. Board of Education, 347 U.S. 483 (1954).

Brown v. Board of Education of Topeka, Kansas, 349 U.S. 294 (1955).

Buchanan v. Warley, 245 U.S. 60 (1917).

Corrigan v. Bulkley, 271 U.S. 323 (1926).

Guinn v. U.S., 238 U.S. 347 (1915).

Harmon v. Taylor, 273 U.S. 668 (1926).

Hitchman Coal and Coke Company v. Mitchell, 254 U.S. 229 (1917).

United Mine Workers of America v. Red Jacket Consolidated Coal and Coke Company, 18F.2d 839 (1927).

KENNETH W. GOINGS is Associate Professor and Chair of the History Department at Rhodes College.